RCMP

THE MARCH WEST

This book is published as part
of the celebration of the 125th
Anniversary of the founding of the
Royal Canadian Mounted Police,
featuring the North-West Mounted
Police March West of 1874.

Produced by:
John McQuarrie Photography

Text Copyright© 1999 Fred Stenson
Design: Dave O'Malley, Aerographics
Layout: Diane Donaldson, Aerographics
Printing: Friesens Corporation,
    Altona, Manitoba

Canadian Cataloguing in
Publication Data

Stenson, Fred, 1951-
RCMP : the march west

ISBN 0-9685071-0-7

1. North West Mounted Police (Canada)–
History. 2. Northwest, Canadian–History–1870-1905.
I. Title.

FC3216.2.S85 1999 362.2'0971 C99-900349-6
HV8157.S78 1999

Published by GAPC Entertainment Inc.
14 Colonnade Road, Suite 250
Nepean, Ontario
Canada K2E 7M6
Tel:(613) 723-3316
Fax: (613) 723-8583
email: www.gapc.com

Printed in Canada

GAPC ENTERTAINMENT INC.
Publisher of the

RCMP
THE MARCH WEST

NWMP • RCMP
1873 - 1999

GAPC gratefully acknowledges the generous
participation and support of the following people
and organizations for their assistance in the
creative design and printing of this book.

Publishers
Marcel H.Clément
Kenneth Stewart

Original Photographs
John McQuarrie Photography

Additional Photographs
Richard Venasse
Christine Bisson
David Walters

Text & Captions
Fred Stenson

Photo Research
William O'Farrell
Fern Graham
Hoda Elatawi

Publicity & Editing
Margery Leach

Design
David O'Malley, Aerographics

Layout
Diane Donaldson, Aerographics

RCMP Coordinator
Greg Peters

RCMP Content Advisors
Dr. Bill Beahen
Allen Burchill,
Assistant Commissioner (Retired)
Glenn Wright

NWMP paintings
Robert Magee

James Lumbers paintings
James Lumbers Publishing Ltd.

Period Maps
Art Director - Kathi Atkinson
Designer - David Badour

Archival Sources
Glenbow Museum
Library & Archives, Calgary

Hudson Bay Archives, Manitoba

Montana Historical Society,
Montana

National Archives of Canada,
Ottawa

National Library of Canada,
Ottawa

The Provincial Archives
of Alberta

Public Archives of Manitoba

Published by
GAPC Entertainment Inc.

In Association with the Royal
Canadian Mounted Police

**With the generous
participation of:**
History Television
Millennium Bureau of Canada
Panasonic Canada Inc.

GAPC March West Website
Address:
rcmpmarchwest.com

Royal Canadian
Mounted Police

Gendarmerie royale
du Canada

G A P C
Video • Audio • Interactive

MARCHE VERS L'OUEST
RCMP ∞ GRC
1874 1999
MARCH WEST

HISTORY
TELEVISION

2000
Canada

Panasonic
Broadcast & Television Systems

"The March West"

James Lumbers '98

NWMP patrol near Fort Walsh, 1878.
The lances these troopers are displaying
were adopted to impress the Indians. Today
they survive in the RCMP's Musical Ride.

TABLE OF CONTENTS

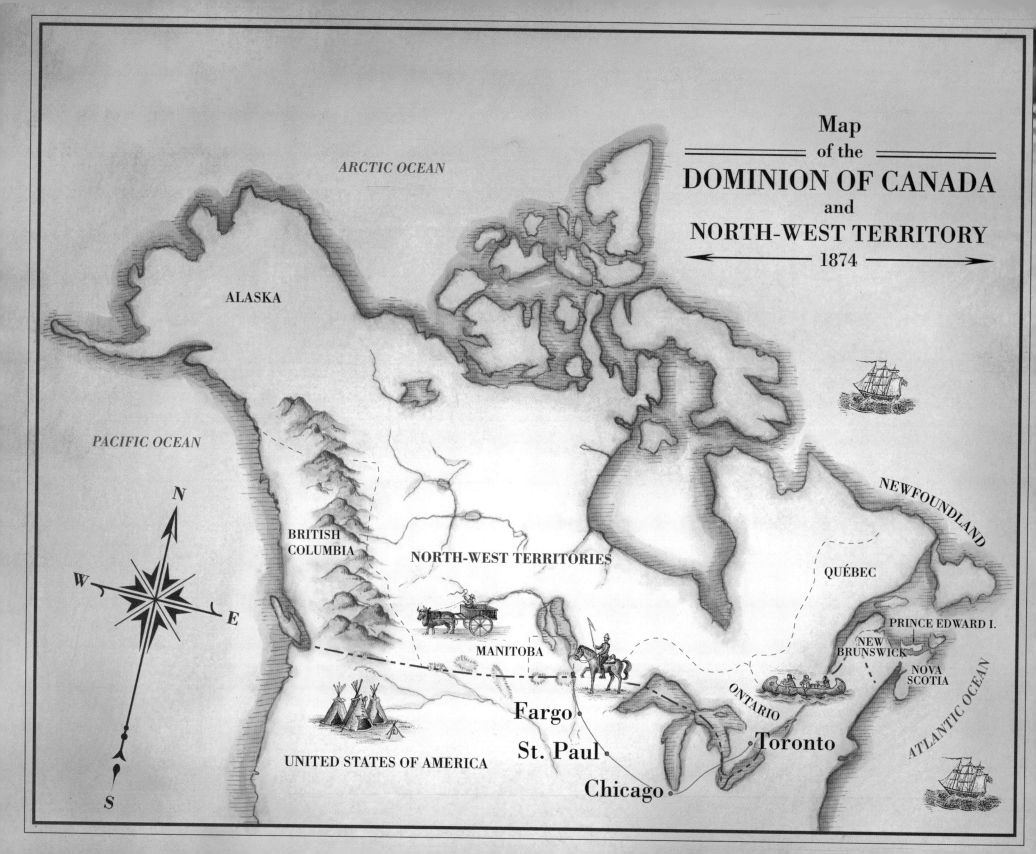

Map
of the
NORTH-WEST TERRITORY
illustrating the
NORTH-WEST MOUNTED POLICE
MARCH WEST
1874

NORTH-WEST TERRITORIES

Ft. Edmonton

N. Saskatchewan R.

Swan R.

L. Manitoba

L. Winnipeg

Red Deer R.

MANITOBA

Lower Ft. Garry

Bow R.

S. Saskatchewan R.

Qu' Appelle R.

Red River

Ft. Ellice

Assiniboine R.

Ft. Macleod

Ft. Whoop-Up

Old Wives L.

Ft. Dufferin

Cypress Hills

Old Wives Creek

Dirt Hills

Roche Percée

Wood Mt.

Sweet Grass Hills

Turtle Mt.

Souris R.

Milk R.

The Missouri Coteau

Red R.

MONTANA TERRITORY

DAKOTA TERRITORY

Ft. Benton

Missouri R.

Fargo

——————— French's route to Sweet Grass Hills

• • • • • • Macleod's route to Ft. Macleod

– – – – – Jarvis's route to Ft. Edmonton

INTRODUCTION

On July 8th, 1874, a mounted police force of 275 men left Fort Dufferin, Manitoba, heading west. Their objective: an American-run whisky trading establishment called Fort Whoop-Up more than 800 miles away. Whoop-Up and several other whisky forts were operating illegally on Canadian soil, a cause of frequent death and much poverty among the people of the Blackfoot Confederacy. The newly minted Canadian mounted police had been created to put a stop to it. In a land area of many millions of acres, they were the law: the sole representatives of Canadian law and order.

The force consisted of clerks, medical students, students of the law, a school teacher, a lawyer, and some railwaymen - but most of the 1874 mounted police were too young to have professions. A few came from military backgrounds, including a Confederate soldier and a veteran of the Crimean War: trained fighters, in other words, rather than guardians of the peace. In a century where military expeditions were regarded as exciting, the common denominator in this disparate group may have been the desire for adventure. Collectively, they knew little about the North-West Territories, as Canada had dubbed the region. In letters and diary entries written before they left the east, they used dime-novel references to Wild Indians, Maidens in Distress, and Fierce Desperados to dream and joke about what lay ahead. Of the true nature of that prairie, they knew next to nothing at all.

There were two well-known trails leading West from Manitoba and, for complex reasons, the mounted police took neither. They split the difference between the two, breaking a trail over treeless hills where the water was both scarce and nearly poisonous when found. When they did locate fresh water, it was only momentary relief because they had no water barrels or individual canteens. Their uniforms were impractical; their weapons obsolete. More than half their horses were unaccustomed to the prairie and unable to thrive on the

10

NORTH-WEST MOUNTED POLICE
THE MARCH WEST

grasses that grew there. Across the west they dragged two field guns weighing more than two ton each. Neither was ever fired at an enemy.

The westward march of the mounted police was, all in all, amazingly ill-planned. Historians are still trying to figure out why. And yet, the march was also a success, much more so than any number of better-planned, better-equipped expeditions in other far corners of the 19th century British Empire, or, for that matter, on the frontiers of the United States. The mounted police set out to stop or slow the whisky trade to the Blackfoot Confederacy and, very soon upon their arrival in the west, they did so. They sought to establish peaceful relations with the First Nations people, and for the most part the chiefs of the Blackfoot Confederacy liked, trusted and approved of them. The force wanted to see the Natives spring back from the poverty the whisky traders had brought them to and, for a time, the Blackfoot did regain prosperity – at least until the buffalo were destroyed and a more severe and less easily resolved poverty took over.

The reason for the surprising success of the mounted police is not to be found in their planning, training, strategy, equipment or skill. The reason existed more in the mind and in the heart.

The simple code of the mounted police was to have one law for everyone, and that, when they made a promise to the First Nations people, they would honour it. They succeeded far better than the United States cavalry because they genuinely did come in peace and mean what they said. As Alberta historian and writer Hugh Dempsey put it, "They came here with the idealistic view that, 'We're going to treat the Indians as equals, we're going to treat the Indians fairly'; and before they could learn from the Americans that this was not the way you do things, their system worked."

From the initial complement of 275 men, the number of Canadian mounted police has risen to over 14,000. Now known as the Royal Canadian Mounted Police (RCMP), the force provides policing to all provinces and territories of Canada except Ontario and Quebec. It also fills police roles on behalf of Canada abroad. The thread of connection that binds this huge, high-tech RCMP to the small disorganized march west of 1874 is the continuing relevance and application of its oldest principles. The RCMP still stands for honesty and one law, applied fairly and equally to all. These ideas, borne west by a handful of mounted police officers in the summer and fall of 1874, have become the RCMP's reputation and proud legend around the world.

THE GREAT LONE LAND

When the mounted police left Manitoba for the far west in July of 1874, they may have thought they were entering a place of emptiness and lawlessness, without human organization, tradition or history. The English soldier and novelist William Butler was sent to conduct a reconnaissance of the area in 1869. He titled his book about the experience The Great Lone Land. Many who may not have read the book took its title as proof that there was nothing much to see or experience west of the Great Lakes. In fact, Butler was sufficiently impressed with the west to write:

"One saw here the world as it had taken shape and form from the hands of the Creator. Nor did the scene look less beautiful because nature alone tilled the earth, and the unaided sun brought forth the flowers."

William Bulter

Before the horse, Natives of the plains moved on foot. Dogs carried their goods.

Native lodges were arranged in a semi-circle, doorways to the rising sun.

The First Nations word for horse was "elk dog." As big as an elk. Able to do the hauling work of a dog.

The mounted police came west to halt the whisky trade that was impoverishing the First Nations people.

The truth about the North-West Territories was that, although the region was lightly populated by Eastern Canadian standards, it was nonetheless populated, and had been for thousands of years. From the time of the last Ice Age, the ancestors of the First Nations people had been surviving, and often thriving, on the prairies, in the parklands, and in the boreal forests of what would eventually become western Canada. For most of their time here, they had been hunting the buffalo on foot, by herding them into pounds and over cliffs: a process that required detailed knowledge of the land and of the buffalo, as well as patience, flawless planning and the total cooperation of the community. It also required what modern religions call faith in that much of their knowledge was encoded in spiritual practices.

As Peigan elder Reg Crowshoe says of his ancestors: "They might have followed the buffalo, but they had a form of government and social control. They knew what authority was. They knew what leadership was."

The arrival of Europeans on the shores of North America brought many changes to the lives of the First Nations people. From the south came the horse, which they called an "elk dog" because it did the hauling work of a dog while being the size of an elk. From south and east came the gun which they called the "thunderstick"

With the horse, First Nations communities traveled farther and faster. They could own more goods.

because, to quote Reg Crowshoe, it "threw rocks that went right through people and killed them." As white traders lured the Natives to forts on the edge of the prairie, Natives were also introduced to "berry water," alcoholic drink that seemed to imbue the drinker with such mad courage that none of his enemies could face him without fear.

The results were a mixture of good and bad. Axes, metal cooking pots and metal scrapers no doubt eased the lives of First Nations women. Excellent use of the horse and the gun increased the ability of Native hunters to kill buffalo. But together with ease and prosperity came European diseases and the murderous chaos that entered the camps after a rum or whisky trade. As memory, tradition, spirituality and cooperation were less critical to hunting the buffalo, some of the traditions faded. As Reg Crowshoe describes it, "There was splitting. Our power of leadership in oral culture had no more power."

The whisky trade may have been the most negative influence of all. In the short run, it caused deaths by misadventure, murder and revenge; in the long run, it steadily impoverished the people to the point where they had few horses or weapons with which to hunt or protect themselves in war. The Blackfoot Confederacy which once had been so prosperous and powerful was becoming weak and poor.

14

Even before the "thunderstick," the horse revolutionized the buffalo hunt.

Robert Magee

As seen in this Blackfoot camp, horse-age tipis were much larger than those formerly hauled by dogs.

THE MÉTIS

The 19th century Métis were descendents of the fur trade. Many Red River Métis were hired as carters, wagon drivers and guides for the March West.

The fur trade that introduced the gun and other products of European technology also created a new indigenous race of people: the Métis. In the 1700s, fur trading companies from Montreal, usually Scottish-owned with French Canadian employees, drove their commerce into the west along the circuitry of rivers. The Hudson's Bay Company (HBC) had received a charter from England's King Charles II in 1692 to trade in all the lands drained by Hudson's Bay. The HBC employed Scottish, Orkney and English men and conducted its training from forts along the shores of Hudson's Bay. In 1774, after it became obvious that the inland-trading Montrealers were harvesting the furs before they could get to the Bay, the HBC moved inland as well, countering the trade of the Montrealers wherever they set up shop.

As there were almost no white women in the fur trading country, by far the majority of children fathered by the fur traders were of First Nations and Métis mothers. The children went to work for the fur trading companies so that eventually the majority of employees in the fur trade were Métis. The term Métis initially meant people of French-Native background, while English, Scottish and Orkney mixed bloods were called "Halfbreeds." In relatively recent times, the word Halfbreed has been dropped because of its racist implications, and people of part-Native ancestry are generally called Métis. Over many generations, the Métis people developed a distinct culture with musical, decorative and sporting traditions all their own.

In the second decade of the 1800s, competition between the Montreal-based Northwest Company and the English Hudson's Bay Company escalated into a violent fur war. Though Métis people worked and fought on both sides, the North-West Company was able to utilize the growing Métis nationalism to further its own cause. In 1821, the two exhausted companies ended the war by amalgamating under the Hudson's Bay Company name.

As with corporate mergers today, the amalgamation of the two largest fur trading concerns in British North America resulted in massive lay-offs. No group was as strongly affected as the Métis. The unemployed and their families were turned out of the fur forts and, while some remained inland to hunt privately or on

After a corporate merger in the fur trade in 1821, Red River (Winnipeg) became the center of Métis life.

The engravings above are two of several that appeared with a Harper's Monthly article about the Red River Métis in 1859.

contract for the HBC, a greater number went to live at the Red River settlement. Begun in 1812 as a new home for exiled Scottish crofters, Red River became a predominantly Métis settlement. The way in which the Métis dealt with the problem of living independently of the fur trade made them a still more organized and politicized group. They freighted, trapped, hunted and farmed and, twice every summer, went to the plains with an enormous cavalcade of ox-drawn Red River carts to hunt the buffalo. The structure of leadership and the strictly enforced rules that governed this hunt, and protected it in the event of attack by Indians, became the basis of Métis self-government.

John A. Macdonald became Canada's first Prime Minister in 1867.

Louis Riel became leader of the Red River Métis in 1869.

The next major events that shaped the character of the west came in the 1860s. First, and not overly important to the west initially, Canada became a nation independent of Britain in 1867. In 1868, the Hudson's Bay Company sold its exclusive charter in North America back to Britain for land and cash, and Britain turned around and gave those rights to Canada. Sir John A. Macdonald, first Prime Minister of Canada, wanted a nation sea-to-sea and, with the acquisition of what Canada called the North-West Territories, that dream was all but realized – provided he could meaningfully govern the west.

The Cree hand sign for "Métis" was two circles (cart wheels) and a line from the right side of the head down the middle of the body.

The Red River Métis rebelled against Canadian authority in 1869, electing their own Provisional Government (pictured above). Louis Riel, their leader, is at the center of the middle row.

One of Canada's first attempts to govern in the North-West Territories, a surveying expedition to Red River, met with rebellion and disaster. When the Red River Métis saw that the Canadian surveyors were ignoring their traditional river lots, a group led by Louis Riel confronted the surveyors. Riel put his foot on the surveyors' chain and said they would go no farther. The resistance escalated and the Métis seized control of the settlement, occupying Fort Garry (the old HBC seat of government), and forming a provisional government with Louis Riel as their leader. After an Orangeman named Thomas Scott was executed, Canada sent a military expedition west under Colonel Garnet Wolseley's command. The Métis leadership fled before this army and Canada attempted once again to govern. In 1871 the Province of Manitoba was created.

In the late 1860s, when Montana traders started building forts on the Canadian side of the 49th Parallel and trading whisky to Blackfoot Confederacy Indians, Canada finally had a cause in the West that was fairly straightforward. The whisky traders had no legitimate business in Canada, and their illegal enterprise was causing a lot of harm. They were there because their own government had outlawed the sale of whisky to Indians and because Canada had not been able to reach the western half of its prairie with either government or law. The whisky traders were essentially thumbing their noses at Canada, and for several years, 1868 to 1873, Canada took the insult without response.

The response when it did come was an Act of Canadian Parliament, passed on May 23rd 1873, to create a mounted force that could police the west. The force's first job would be to send the American whisky traders packing and to restore peace and order among the First Nations people.

RAISING THE FORCE

The Canadian mounted police force was the brain child of Prime Minister Sir John A. Macdonald. As a nation-builder Macdonald needed to hold onto the region between the Great Lakes and the Rocky Mountains against the threat of possible American expansion. He intended to string the parts of Canada together with a railway and to cover its western prairie with settlers. First the region had to be secured and pacified. Macdonald proposed a force of mounted riflemen who would ride west, put down the whisky trade and befriend the Indians.

Sir John A. Macdonald's model for this police force was the Royal Irish Constabulary: cavalry trained to rifle and artillery; a "police-styled" force but with a military bearing. The mounted police would be more like an army when enforcing Canadian sovereignty along the border, and more like police when arresting domestic law breakers. That the police be like police and not like an army was particularly important because of the experience the Blackfoot Confederacy and other tribes were having with the U.S. Cavalry: the hated "blue coats." Only four years earlier, U.S. Colonel Eugene Baker and 300 U.S. Cavalry had attacked a camp of Peigan (Blackfoot Confederacy) Indians on the Marias River. Baker and his men wiped out the camp, leaving 173 men, women and children dead; an atrocity made only slightly worse by the facts that the Peigan were helpless with smallpox at the time, and weren't even the Indians Baker had been told to "punish."

The Canadian force was designed not to act, nor to look, like the "blue coats." This was one of the major reasons for their scarlet jackets.

21

"No person shall be appointed to the Police Force unless he be of a sound constitution, able to ride, active and able-bodied, of good character and between the ages of eighteen and forty years; nor unless he be able to read and write either the English or French language."

Act of Parliament, 1873

In this way, the Canadian mounted police force was designed on paper. The event that transformed them into reality was another atrocity, this time on Canadian soil: an event known to history as the Cypress Hills Massacre. It started with a group of Canadian and American "wolfers" (wolf hunters and poisoners) who had their horses stolen by Indians while returning to Fort Benton, Montana from a hunting expedition in Canada. Blackfoot Indians stole the horses and chased them into the Cypress Hills before doubling back west to give the impression the horses had been stolen by the Cree or Assiniboine. The ruse worked and the wolfers followed the trail into the Cypress Hills, winding up at Abe Farwell's and Moses Solomon's whisky forts, where a large group of Assiniboine Indians were drinking heavily after completing a trade. Angry at not finding their horses, the wolfers started drinking too. On June 1st, 1873, a horse belonging to one of the forts' employees went briefly missing and the wolfers used it as an excuse to attack the Assiniboine. They killed all the men, women and children they could, a number believed to be more than one hundred. Upon their return to Fort Benton, they were hailed by the public and the local press.

It took some time for this news to make its way to eastern Canada and, when it did, the story was slightly at odds with the facts. It was reported that American whisky traders (rather than Canadian and American wolfers) had killed the Assiniboine and the effect was to turn the Government opposition and the Canadian public into loud advocates for recruiting and sending the mounted police west as soon as possible. The first three Divisions (A, B and C), 150 men in all, were hastily recruited and put aboard boats on the Great Lakes before freeze-up in the fall of 1873. Debarking at Prince Arthur's Landing (near Thunder Bay), they marched over the Dawson Route to Lower Fort Garry. It was by all reports an awful journey, wet and cold. After one particularly cold night, a large quantity of provisions froze down so solidly it had to be abandoned.

23

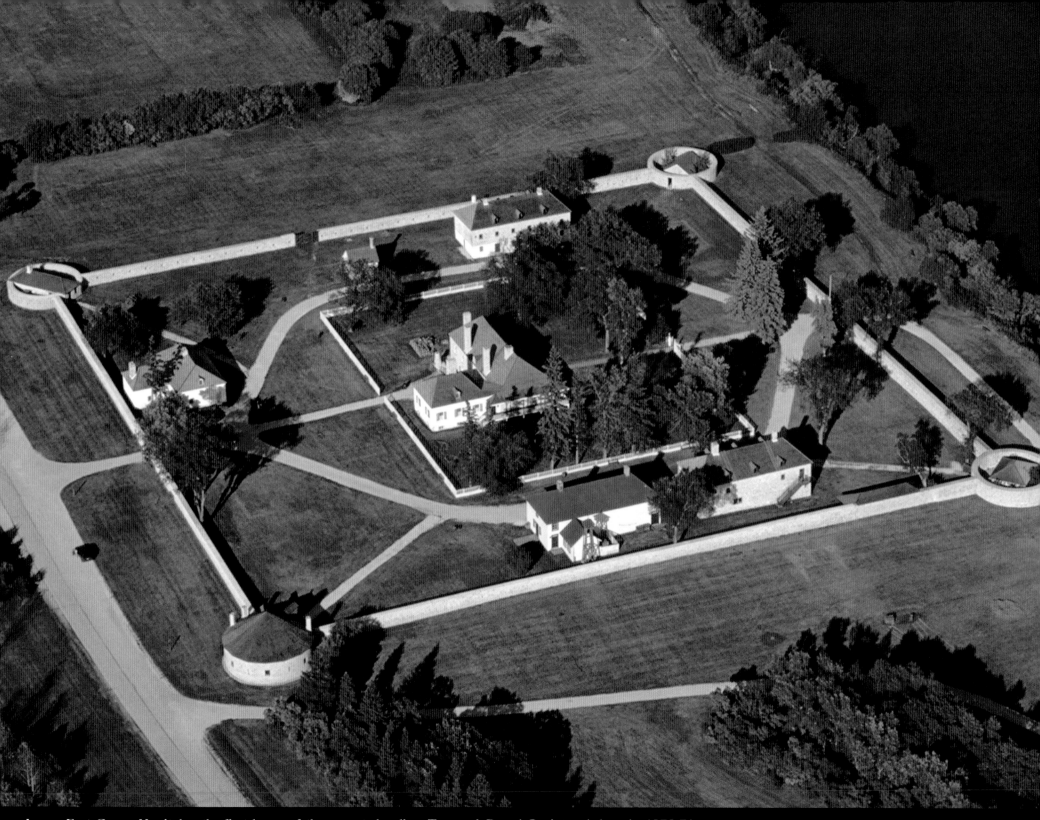

Lower Fort Garry, Manitoba; the first home of the mounted police. Troops A,B and C wintered there in 1873-74.

THE COMMISSIONER

George Arthur French: first Commissioner
of the Canadian Mounted Police.

After arrival at Lower Fort Garry (down river from the Red River settlement), the first men were sworn in on November 3rd. Three days later the Macdonald government fell over the Pacific Scandal (a scandal over the financing of Sir John A.'s railway). Liberal Alexander Mackenzie, a temperance advocate, took over as Prime Minister, and took over as well the problem of getting the mounted police into action against the whisky traders.

One of Sir John A.'s last actions with respect to the mounted police was to name the first Commissioner of the force. Macdonald had wanted someone with British credentials, preferably from the Royal Irish Constabulary, or perhaps with experience in India. Out of the candidates, the closest to meeting the criteria was Colonel George Arthur French, a Roscommon Irishman who had briefly served in the Royal Irish Constabulary as a young man. French was a captain in Britain's Royal Artillery, seconded to the School of Artillery in Kingston, Ontario as an acting Lieutenant-Colonel. A strict disciplinarian with a cool and stiff demeanor, he had very little experience commanding in the field. He badly wanted the job of Commissioner as it would correct this inexperience and pave the way to greater promotions.

In the winter of 1873-74, Colonel French traveled to Lower Fort Garry to have a look at the 150 men who were training there. He did not much like what he saw. Several recruits were medically unfit and would have to be discharged. Others would be discharged for gambling and drinking. French was a connoisseur of horses and the part-prairie mustangs on which Sergeant-Major Sam Steele was training the men seemed of very low quality to French. Many were probably spotted horses or paints in an age when British and European horsemen regarded the solid-coloured horse as naturally superior to piebald varieties.

25

The first commissioner of the NWMP, Lieutenant-Colonel French cut an imposing figure. The spectacular visual traditions of red serge and gold stripe had their roots in his impressive military bearing.

Robert Magee

When Colonel French returned to Ottawa, he pleaded with the government for the other 150 men provided for in the Act. At length he got his wish and Troops D, E and F were born. He took an active part in the recruitment of the new men and in the purchase of their horses. He preferred men from military backgrounds (or at least with militia experience) and horses of well-bred appearance that would impress the Indians and whisky traders.

Sergeant Major Sam Steele: the mounted police riding instructor at Lower Fort Garry.

Troops D, E and F, recruited in the spring of 1874, trained at New Fort, Toronto (pictured above).

In a frenzied month, the recruits were drilled at New Fort in Toronto, and the drill sergeants soon learned that most of them had significantly exaggerated their ability to ride. An often told joke at the expense of a fallen recruit was for the Sergeant-Major to bawl: "Who gave you permission to dismount, sir?"

Troops D, E and F boarded the train at Union Station on June 6th, 1874, with a brass band playing and tearful families bidding them farewell. The event was less splendid than it might have been because the train would shortly enter the United States where the men were forbidden to carry arms or wear their uniforms. The striking scarlet jackets were back in the baggage cars, as was the weaponry.

Sleeping arrangements in the officers' car on the train from Toronto to Fargo, North Dakota (as drawn by Henri Julien).

The police were accompanied on the train by a young civilian, a Montreal artist/reporter working for the Canadian Illustrated News. Colonel French had contacted the newspaper and offered free passage, rations and a horse to a reporter if they would send one along. The newspaper's choice was Henri Julien, just 21 years old, a printer's son from Quebec City. Julien's early reports described thousands of hogs in the Chicago stockyards and a hospitable reception in the city of St. Paul. When they reached rail's end at Fargo, North Dakota on June 12th, and stood on the little platform facing out on limitless prairie, he was moved to write:

"Behind us lay the works of man, with their noises; before us stretched the handiwork of God."

The Canadian Illustrated News, Canada's leading picture periodical, was asked by Colonel French to send a reporter/illustrator on the March West.

MOVING OUT

Fort Dufferin (today's Emerson, Manitoba) was built for the International Boundary Commission that surveyed the western half of the Canada/United States border in 1873 and '74.

The six original Troops of the mounted police met at Fort Dufferin in June of 1874 to prepare for the March West.

Six Troops of mounted police, the three at Lower Fort Garry and Colonel French's three at Fargo, were scheduled to rendezvous at Fort Dufferin in southern Manitoba. But Colonel French could not immediately move out in that direction because his wagons and harnesses came off the train in poorly sorted pieces. After a masterwork of assembly, it was time to harness the eastern horses. They were saddle horses that had never before felt a harness strap or a horse collar and the resulting mayhem was unavoidable.

Besides the rebellion of some of the horses, the chaos owed as well to the fact that most men had exaggerated their ability to ride, and the brief training at New Fort had not remedied that deficit. But even more disquieting for Colonel French had to be seeing how rapidly his eastern horses failed over this relatively short journey of 160 miles. Two of them died. Horses cannot be changed over from eastern forage to prairie grass and immediately thrive. According to experts it can take as much as a year for a horse to adapt. Colonel French did not know this and was learning the hard way.

Fred Bagley, seen here in his twenties, was 15 years old when he served on the March West as a trumpeter.

As French moved north, Colonel James F. Macleod, the Assistant Commissioner, was on his way south from Lower Fort Garry with Divisions A, B and C. The winter he had just passed at Lower Fort Garry was not Macleod's first time in the west. He had been here with Wolseley's army in 1870, and that additional experience seemed to make Macleod more comfortable in command than was his superior officer. The diaries and memoirs of the men are certainly kinder to Macleod than they are to French, perhaps because Macleod fitted in more easily with the enlisted men and laborers, and because he wasn't so directly identifiable as the cause of their problems and discomforts.

On June 19th, a day after Macleod's arrival at Fort Dufferin, Colonel French and his men rolled in, and the six Divisions were together in one place for the first time. Looking back at his experience as a fifteen year old trumpeter on the force, Fred Bagley remembered that day as a joyous one, more so than the next day when nature decided to demonstrate its prairie power.

An electrical storm struck the mounted police camp at Fort Dufferin on the night of June 20th, 1874.

On the night of June 20th, as the camp was settling in the for the night, the skies ignited. A prairie storm blew in and showered the camp with rain and bolts of lightning. As a precaution the eastern horses had been picketed inside the square of tents and wagons, but when a lightning bolt struck among them, the horses tore from the picket line and surged round the enclosure looking for any way of escape. Sergeant Major Sam Steele, the Lower Fort Garry riding instructor, remembered the scene to the end of his life:

"The maddened beasts overturned the huge wagons, dashed through a row of tents, scattered everything. In their mad efforts to pass, they climbed over one another to a height of many feet."

Sam Steele

Robert Magee's painting "Stampede." The panicked horses fled Ft. Dufferin and ran for sixty miles.   Robert Magee

The "inferior" prairie cayuses did not join the stampede, allowing Sam Steele, Sub-Inspector James Walker, young Fred Bagley and other of the better riders, to mount up and give chase. They rode south all night, their way lit by the lightning that did not stop until 6 A.M. By then they were back in North Dakota, sixty miles from the Dufferin camp. Within 24 hours, the men and horses were back at Fort Dufferin again, all thoroughly exhausted. Fred Bagley arrived asleep in his saddle and did not wake as Inspector James Walsh picked him off his horse and carried him to bed. Of the 250 horses that joined the stampede, only one was lost.

It was an ominous beginning, especially for Colonel French who had been so personally responsible for the choice of horses. It did not help when a local authority from Dufferin suggested that French would be lucky to get back by Christmas with 40% of his horses alive.

Before leaving Fort Dufferin for the prairie, Colonel French made one last attempt to rid himself of the ruffians and cowards in his force. He gathered the men and gave a speech about the trials that awaited them on the trail west. Hunger and thirst were guaranteed, and even death was possible. He as much as invited the weak of heart to desert now while there was time. By the following morning, more than thirty men, including one officer, had taken him at his word. They were gone from camp, legging it as fast possible for the U.S. border.

Several mounties were injured during the stampede.

Robert Magee's "The March."

Robert Magee

The March West left Fort Dufferin on July 8th, 1874.

On July 8th, 1874 the expedition was finally ready. At 5 PM that day they moved out. They were in their dress uniforms for the occasion - scarlet jackets, grey trousers, pillbox hats or snow white pith helmets, white gauntlet gloves and shining black riding boots. Each division rode a different colour of horse: dark bays for "A" Division, dark browns for "B," and so on. Behind the riders came nine-pounder field guns on their limbers, the wagons and Métis ox-carts piled high with provisions, the mowing machines and, finally, the cattle (Colonel French's beef on the hoof).

The route the expedition would take had been decided before leaving and, in hindsight, many point to it as the primary mistake from which many of the expedition's misfortunes flowed. The best choice would likely have been to take the well-beaten fur trade road from Red River to Fort Edmonton, and then approach Fort Whoop-Up from the north. The second best would have been to follow the trail made by the Boundary Commission which, by 1874, was in the latter stages of surveying the western half of the Canada/U.S. border. But the line of march urged on Colonel French by Ottawa, and by North-West Territories Lt.-Governor Alexander Morris, was a third option. French was to follow the Boundary Commission road for 200 miles. Then, because of warfare between the Sioux and the American army just south of the border, he would veer northwest into the Missouri Coteau hills. When he had put a comfortable distance between himself and the border, he could resume travel westward toward Fort Whoop-Up. Beyond that first 200 miles, the route made no sense at all. The country was dry, steep, trackless and barren. The water was scarce and alkaline when found. Nonetheless, those were French's orders.

35

The march followed the Boundary Commission road for the first 200 miles. In this photo of Boundary Commission employees, L.W. Herchmer is 4th from the left at back. Herchmer became Mounted Police Commissioner in 1886.

Although the worst would come when the expedition left the road, the first 200 miles were no picnic either. For some reason, when equipping the expedition, Colonel French had operated under the belief that there would be sufficient water all along the way. Hence, he did not bother to include water barrels or personal canteens. Very soon into the journey, between river crossings, the men and animals were forced to drink stagnant slough water. The line of men on sick parade grew longer by the day, most suffering from dysentery. Two men contracted typhoid fever and had to be taken back to Dufferin. The horses also suffered from the bad water. Combined with their difficulties digesting "prairie wool", many of the horses were soon too weak to use.

Besides these problems, Colonel French often confided in his diary a deep frustration over the way the freight wagons, ox-carts and cattle lagged behind. Sometimes his line of march stretched to a totally indefensible ten miles in length. He tended to blame the Métis carters, who he saw as lazy and inclined to ignore his orders, and their Red River carts which he described as a vehicle more suited to the 1st century than to the 19th. The shrieking noise that the carts' ungreased wheel hubs made was a cause of complaint among most of the men.

Colonel French's criticism of the Red River cart was neither fair, nor correct. In truth, the cart was very well adapted to prairie travel. The two huge wheels made for deep clearance over ruts and rocks. Its all-wood and leather construction meant it could always be repaired without need of metal or a forge. When the rivers were in flood, the whole thing could be dismantled and refashioned into a buffalo-skin covered boat. Even the shrieking wheel hubs were a product of someone's wisdom. Grease might have made the carts quieter but would have trapped stones and caused breakage.

Colonel French despised the Red River cart for its slowness.

Actor portraying Colonel French.

The Métis cart drivers knew that an ox will travel at its own speed.

Red River cart was made entirely of wood and leather.
It could be quickly dismantled and floated across rivers.

The speed of a Red River cart was the speed of an ox - never fast - and the Metis drivers were masters at going no faster than the animal could without losing weight and threatening its health.

Colonel French did not understand this, nor did he originally realize that cattle cannot travel as fast as men on horseback. In the end, in an attempt to hurry up the carters and drovers, he sent his policemen back to help with the driving. The men saw cart and wagon driving as vastly below their dignity, and this it became one of the most unpopular orders given on the march.

As they pushed on across the prairie, French's eastern horses continued to fail and, on July 22nd, he issued another greatly unpopular order. This time it was to tell the men, whether they were riding a horse or on a wagon, that they must walk every second hour. Sergeant Major Smythe, found at rest among the pots and pans of a cook wagon, simply refused. He had joined a mounted force, was his explanation to Colonel French, not a walking one. In a rare disciplinary lapse, French let him ride.

One result of making the men walk was that their riding boot leather began rapidly to wear out. By the end of the march, many would be walking with their feet bound in sacks.

The Métis worked for the March West both as carters and as guides.

Robert Magee

On July 22nd, Colonel French ordered the mounted policemen and drivers to walk every second hour to save the horses.

On July 24th, the expedition reached a wind-carved limestone formation called Roche Percée. Just beyond it was the confluence of Rivière Courte and the Souris River. The wood, pasture and water were all good here and Colonel French called the first lengthy halt. For five days he let the men and animals rest while he himself implemented a plan to split the force into two parts. Before he entered the no man's land of the Missouri Coteau, he wanted rid of the weak, the sick and the slow. Given what lay ahead, it was not a bad decision.

Henri Julien's
drawing of
Roche Percée.

On July 24th, the March reached the wind-carved limestone formation called Roche Percée.

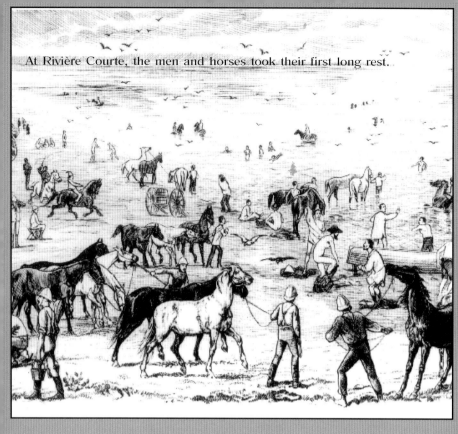

At Rivière Courte, the men and horses took their first long rest.

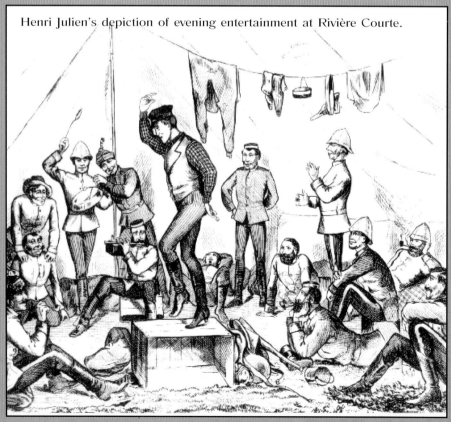

Henri Julien's depiction of evening entertainment at Rivière Courte.

The mounted police camp near Roche Percée (July 24th - 29th) took on a festival atmosphere. The men bathed and washed their clothes in the river. At night, an ad hoc band of fife, spoons and drum provided accompaniment for bawdy and sentimental songs. Meanwhile, Colonel French was in his tent working out the details of whom and what to send to Forts Ellice and Edmonton with Inspector W.D. Jarvis and "A" Troop. Jean D'Artigue, a young school teacher from France, was one of those selected from other Divisions to go with Inspector Jarvis. He was extremely critical in his memoir of French's motives and tactics. First, Colonel French took all the sick men, weak horses and slowest carts and cattle and gave them to "A" Troop. Then he took many of "A" Division's best horses and distributed them among the other Troops that would be continuing west. There is no doubt Colonel French was lightening his load and seeking to speed up his progress by these moves, but he did not exactly leave "A" Division helpless. Inspector Jarvis was a capable officer and Sergeant Major Steele, who also accompanied "A" Troop, would have been a definite asset in the possible battle for Fort Whoop-Up. The worst off of Jarvis's men and horses would be left at Fort Ellice so that "A" Division's longest haul, up to Fort Edmonton, would be made by the strongest men and animals he had. There was also the fact that Colonel French would soon be leaving the commission road and heading into unknown country. Those suffering from illness and fatigue were better off away from that foray.

INTO THE UNKNOWN

On August 4th, the mounted police left the Boundary Commission road and entered unmarked territory

A Métis buffalo hunter.

Robert Magee

Ten days earlier, on July 14th, six Métis guides from Red River had joined the column. They and several wagons full of gifts for the Indians had been sent by Lt.-Governor Morris to help Colonel French and his mounted police along their way. The Métis guides were led by a Herculean figure named Pierre Léveillé, about whom Henri Julien enthused. Pierre Léveillé and the other Métis guides were, according to Julien, "worth, in sagacity and endurance, any twenty of our own men." When Colonel French left the Boundary Commission road on August 4th for a trackless climb to the summit of the Missouri Coteau, or "Dirt Hills," he needed the help of his guides badly - and he found them suddenly unable to tell him much of anything. The Red River Métis were mostly descended from the Cree and Ojibwa people and, as the police struggled up the Coteau hills, the Métis were moving out of their familiar territory into enemy country. In 1851, the Red River Métis buffalo hunt had encountered the Sioux when hunting on the Coteau and, though they won the ensuing battle and the Sioux had asked for peace, it was still a reminder that the Métis were best off to stay east of the country of the Sioux and Blackfoot. As a result, the Red River guides did not know the country they were entering, and Colonel French was left largely to his own devices - a prismatic compass set and a wheel odometer.

A mounted police scout.

Robert Magee

The March West included no draft horses. Saddle horses pulled the field guns that some men called "horse killers."

Robert Magee

When the horses could no longer pull the field guns, oxen and men took over.

Another difficulty on the climb into the Coteau hills was pulling the two 9-pound field guns. Colonel French had already arrested two of his officers for their insubordinate opinions about his use of saddle horses to pull field guns and other freight. On the Dirt Hills, those arguments must have echoed in his mind as he watched the horses work themselves near to death trying to get the two-ton field pieces to the summit. Finally, the horses could not make the climb and the power of oxen and men was employed. When they did reach the summit, an estimated 1,000 feet above the rest of the prairie, the expedition was suffering badly from fatigue. The one consolation was that a large expanse of water glimmered in the distance: Old Wives Lake. When they reached the water on August 8th, they found it thick with alkali. It smelled like weeds soaked in brine. Once again, the men and animals gave in to their thirst and drank anyway, with the usual purgative consequences.

Another feature of the climb into the Dirt Hills was that the expedition's artist went missing. Bored with the monotony of the prairie, Henri Julien had gone duck hunting with one of the guides. When they found a lake and some ducks, Julien struck off on his own and, in his excitement over bringing down a couple of birds, he let go of his horse. The cayuse, "Rooster," wouldn't let Julien catch him again. For the entire day, Rooster ran a few steps ahead of Julien. By the time Julien did catch him, it was dark. Julien had no choice but to put his head on his saddle and sleep under the stars. The artist slept so soundly that he missed both a flare and a blast from the field gun ignited for him by Colonel French.

THE NORTH-WEST EXPEDITION : OUR SPECIAL ARTIST AND HIS HORSE "OLD ROOSTER" LOST ON THE PRAIRIE

1. Out Hunting
2. Game
3. A race after Old Rooster.
4. Away again to the setting sun.
5. Not finding the trail, took a sleep.
6. Next morning : Old Rooster off again.
7. Signals : Friends on the search.
8. Found
9. Why, where you been?

This 9-panel drawing by Henri Julien depicts his duck hunting adventure in early August. While hunting, Julien let his horse get away. By the time he caught him, it was too late to return to camp and Julien slept under the stars. Next morning, "Rooster," his horse, got away again. That day, to everyone's relief, the artist was found by a search party.

THE SICKEST AND THE WEAKEST

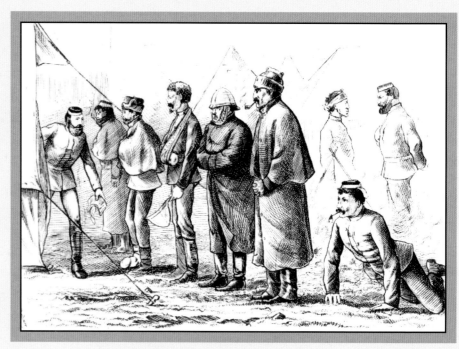

The physicians, Dr. Kittson (pictured in his tent above left) and his assistant Dr. Nevitt, were kept busy
on the March West. When the men had no choice but to drink bad water, the evening sick parade grew long.

Julien and a search party found each other next morning and the artist was proud to report "manifestations of joy" at his reappearance.

Beyond Old Wives Lake, the expedition found better pasture, water and wood at Old Wives Creek on August 11th. Colonel French declared the spot his "Cripple Camp." Again, he would leave the sickest and the weakest men and horses behind.

At the Old Wives Creek Cripple Camp, the expedition encountered its first Indians: a small encampment of Sisseton Sioux. Historian

Hugh Dempsey believes the meeting was largely accidental, and a cause of some worry on both sides. The mounted police had heard many stories about the fierce and warlike Sioux. The Sioux could not be certain at a glance if the mounties were peaceful or more like the U.S. cavalry with whom their people had long been at war. As groups foreign to one another will often do in moments of mutual distrust, they resorted to formality and pomp, staging a Pow-Wow. The Sioux danced for the mounted policemen, and the leaders on both sides shared the pipe of peace. Several speeches were made and they parted on good terms.

Pow-wow with the Sisseton Sioux at Old Wives Creek: the first time the police met Native people on the March West.

Before leaving this camp, Colonel French was confronted by a wild looking trapper. The man's name was Morrow (some give it as Morin or Morriseau) and he claimed to know the country ahead, having trapped on the Bow River for a season. Colonel French considered Morrow "a hard case" and did not like nor trust him. It was all too likely that he was a spy sent by the whisky traders to confuse him. But, given the serious inadequacy of the scouts he did have, French could not simply turn the man away. French and Sub-Inspector Walker had been surveying by the sun, and by the stars every night, but the Palliser Expedition map they were using was not precise. They still could not be absolutely sure where they were with respect to any landmark. Finally, French did hire Morrow, but resolved to keep a close eye on him.

In this scene from "The Great March," the Mounties are shown riding among aspens. Between wooded sections, they often rode for days without wood, burning

"buffalo chips" for fuel.

Prior to Roche Percée, the expedition had always had wood to burn for fuel. The last depot on the Boundary Commission road before they left it was called Wood End, and it meant what it said. From there onward, there were no trees and the men were forced to cook with dried buffalo dung, or buffalo "chips," for fuel. The chips worked fine and burned hot, except when it rained. When the buffalo chips were wet, it meant a cold camp and no hot food.

By August 28th, the mounted police were marching alongside the Cypress Hills. The hills were an important landmark in many ways. First they were the location of the massacre that had spurred the force into existence in the summer months of 1873. They were also an important territorial divider. Just as the hills divided the Mississippi and Hudson's Bay water-sheds, they also divided the lands of a number of Indian Nations. The Sioux, Assiniboine, Plains Cree, Gros Ventre and Blackfoot Confederacy all hunted here, and to some extent claimed the hills as their own. As a result the Cypress Hills were the site of frequent inter-tribal confrontations.

Passing through the northern edge of the Cypress Hills the expedition took extra precautions at night, such as handing out ammunition to the men and posting extra guards. Though the force had come to this land hoping to improve conditions for the Blackfoot Confederacy, they were not certain of their welcome. Some believed the Blackfoot were under the control of the whisky traders now and might be urged to attack the police on the traders' behalf.

On September 2nd, not long after the expedition entered Blackfoot country, the scouts found buffalo and the men enjoyed a rousing hunt. Colonel French shot two buffalo and the scouts shot another two. Determined not to miss out, Henri Julien entered the chase on Old Rooster. Though he admitted abusing his horse to accomplish the deed, Julien managed to kill a bull. When he was done, the rowels of his spurs were bent and Rooster's flanks streamed with blood.

That day the men ate until they could hold no more. As long as they remained within hunting range of the buffalo, they continued to feast. Although it sounds like a tall tale, the story goes they were eating up to ten pounds of meat per day per man.

That the force had not seen a buffalo from Fort Dufferin until now was a sad testament to the declining numbers of the animal. The herds that had once blackened the prairie for miles were

The police saw and hunted their first buffalo on September 2nd.

now reduced to a few remnant herds, one of the largest of which was north of the Missouri River in Blackfoot territory. These were the last great buffalo herds on earth. The plains Indians and Métis to the east were already dealing with the severe decline of their staple animal. The Blackfoot had that tragedy yet to live.

A few policemen were equipped as lancers, to impress the Natives.

Inspector James Morrow Walsh and "B" Troop cross the South Saskatchewan en route to Fort Edmonton. Later, on the advice of guide Pierre Léveillé, Colonel French called for Walsh and his men to return and continue with the other divisions to the Sweetgrass Hills.

A few days after the first buffalo were shot, Colonel French and his men reached the South Saskatchewan River and the problem with the guides, specifically with the American scout Morrow, reached a crisis. For some days Colonel French had been allowing Morrow to lead the way. He was supposed to be taking them to the confluence of the Belly and Bow Rivers where French had been told he would find Fort Whoop-Up. By comparing Morrow's statements to his own location finding and map, Colonel French finally caught Morrow out in a definite lie. Morrow claimed to have found the confluence 70 miles from where it showed on the map. On closer examination, the river

Morrow claimed was the Bow entering the Belly proved to be no more than a sharp curve in the South Saskatchewan River.

To his diary on September 6th, Colonel French darkly committed the words, "There is not a soul in camp that knows this place." Even their entry into buffalo country had its sinister side-effect. Where a buffalo herd has been, there is often not a blade of grass left and all the water is tramped and fouled. The horses, now barely shades of their former selves, were starving.

At this point, French and his men were wandering lost. To add to their trials, a cold wind and rain set in from the north on September 8th. Next day the storm continued and French sent some of the horses into a ravine for feed and to be out of the wind. When he tried to leave again the horses were so paralyzed with cold they could not climb out of the gully and five of them died within hours. On the 10th, French gave an order for the men to surrender one of their two sleeping blankets and to use it to cover a horse at night. In his diary that day, French worried lest the rain turn to snow. "If a few hours cold rain kills off a number of horses, what would be the effect of a 24 hours' snow storm?"

When his scouts did finally locate the meeting of the Belly and the Bow Rivers, Colonel French realized just how lost he was. All that marked the spot were three abandoned cabins, missing their roofs. Even French's intelligence as to the location of Fort Whoop-Up was wrong.

Colonel French immediately called a meeting of his officers. He had been told various stories along the way and one of them was that the whisky traders were not even at Fort Whoop-Up. As the mounted police approached, the traders

When the mounted police could not find Fort Whoop-Up, they marched south to the Sweetgrass Hills.

were said to have withdrawn to Fort Benton, Montana, content to wait until the mounties had been and gone. As with other stories, French could not know if this one was true or someone's convenient lie, but, in the present circumstance, it suited him to believe and act on it. He decided to forget Fort Whoop-Up for the moment and to concentrate on getting his men and their horses to safety.

At first, Colonel French wanted to take four Divisions south to the Sweetgrass Hills while sending the fifth Division, Inspector Walsh's "B" Troop, north to Fort Edmonton. He got as far as having Walsh and his men ford the river to the Edmonton side before Pierre Léveillé returned from a reconnoiter and strongly advised against it. Léveillé had ridden up the Bow River and there was no grass there. If Inspector Walsh went that way, it was unlikely any of his horses would survive. Colonel French recalled Walsh and, on September 15th, all five divisions made for the Sweetgrass Hills that showed as three buttes on the southern horizon.

This final journey was probably the mounted police's most desperate. Inspector James Walker declared that he had never seen country so bare of grass. The north wind and rain continued.

Trumpeter Bagley recalled seeing men lying on the ground around a muck hole, sucking the cool mud for its bit of moisture. On September 18th, they came to the top of the Milk River Ridge and, for the first time, saw the Rocky Mountains. Remebering the moment, Fred Bagley wrote:

"What a thrilling sight it was to us wandering Ishmaelites! But as we stood there, after months of weary travel, and saw their snow-capped summits glittering in the bright sunlight, while almost at our feet the prairie as far as the eye could see in every direction was covered by countless numbers of buffalo, elk and antelope, the sight was bewildering."

Fred Bagley

Later the same day the marchers reached the west butte of the Sweetgrass Hills. The water and grass were good and there was even coal to fuel the forge. It was a good camp for the men, but for many of the horses it was too late. So many horses died at this camp that the men called it "Dead Horse Coulee."

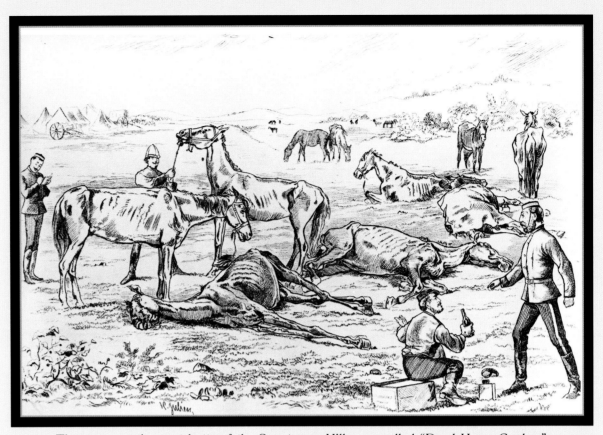

The camp on the west butte of the Sweetgrass Hills was called "Dead Horse Coulee."

A shortage of good water was a continuing problem throughout the march.

In the History Television special "The Great March," Colonel French was played by RCMP Cpl. Jerry McCarty.

Colonel French had made a great many decisions in recent days. He saw the need to return east with some of the men while the majority - if Ottawa would agree to it - would stay, build a fort, and thereby create a permanent obstacle to the return of the whisky traders. Nothing else would stop them.

He had decided that his job was not to pursue the whisky traders himself but to hand that responsibility on to Colonel Macleod while he went east and looked into other matters of importance to the force, such as their winter quarters and their permanent headquarters in the west. He would take with him Divisions "D" and "E" while Colonel Macleod went on to Fort Whoop-Up with Divisions "B," "C," and "F."

What Colonel Macleod would encounter when he finally found Fort Whoop-Up was still anyone's guess. Colonel French's idea that it was empty was just hearsay at this point, and Macleod needed to be ready for a battle, whether there was to be a battle or not.

To make preparations for their now separate missions, the two Colonels, French and Macleod, rode together to Fort Benton. For the feed and provisions they needed, for access to a telegraph, there was no place for them to go except into the home of the whisky trade.

Colonel James Macleod (2nd from the right) stayed in the west with three divisions to permanently halt the whisky trade.

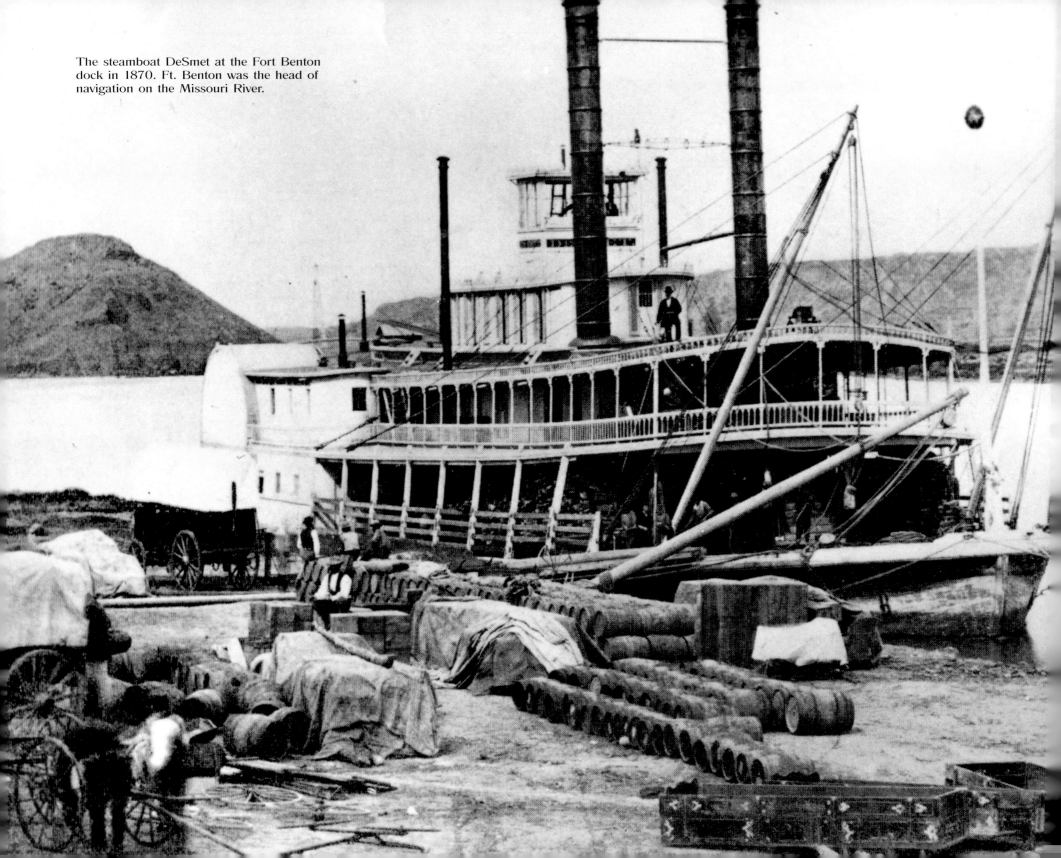

The steamboat DeSmet at the Fort Benton dock in 1870. Ft. Benton was the head of navigation on the Missouri River.

Hauling for outfitters like T.C. Powers and Bros., Fort Benton teamsters drove a well-established road from Benton to Fort Whoop-Up.

On the levée at Fort Benton, whisky came off the steamboats and buffalo hides went on.

FORT WHOOP-UP

In 1874, Fort Benton, Montana was a wild town with a reputation for violence and lawlessness. Originally a trading post for the American Fur Company, it grew rapidly during the 1860s Montana gold rush. Most of the provisions that entered the gold frontier and most of the ore that left it went by steamboat on the Missouri River. Fort Benton was the highest point on the Missouri that the steamboats could reach at that time. When the gold rush cooled, Benton remained the communication and provisioning center for the types of business that continued: prospecting, trapping, trading, buffalo hunting and whisky.

When Colonel French and Colonel Macleod arrived at Fort Benton on September 24th, telegrams from Ottawa awaited them. The federal government had written, accepting Colonel French's plan to leave a strong contingent of mounted policemen on the Belly River under Macleod's command. With that, the way was clear for French to leave Benton, and rejoin Divisions D and E for the trip east.

"Purchased some moccasins, boots, stockings, gloves, & c, for the men and some corn and oats for the horses. Bought 15 horses. Left one with Macleod. Prices generally very low."

Colonel French

French left Fort Benton the following day.

It took Colonel Macleod a bit longer to prepare for the march to Fort Whoop-Up and the upcoming winter on the prairies. Through his eyes Fort Benton was no grand. In a September 28th letter to his future wife, he called the town "a miserable hole," "nothing but 2 stores and a collection of whisky shops."

By the time Colonel Macleod was able to leave Fort Benton, he had in his employ a new man: a half-Blood Indian, half-Scottish scout named Jerry Potts. Small and bow-legged Potts was not impressive to look at but was a legend in this part of the world. One of his more recent exploits was leading a decisive charge in an 1870 battle between the Cree and Blackfoot on the Belly River. The battle had gone on for some time when Potts arrived. First, he began picking off the Cree from long range with his rifle. Then, spying a weak spot in their line of defense, he led the charge, routed the Cree and drove them into the river.

As for whisky, Potts had a considerable taste for it, but had also suffered personal losses for which the whisky trade was responsible. The

v of Fort Whoop-Up. Colonel French brought two field guns in the belief that the whisky traders were well armed. The cannon in this photograph
he was right.

Fort Whoop-Up in its heyday, before the mounted police arrived. What looks like an American flag is actually a trading company flag.

Jerry Potts signaled Macleod and the two of them rode to the main gate of the fort alone. They went inside and were welcomed by Dave Akers, a civil war veteran and trader. There were few others present. Colonel Macleod called for the rest of his men to enter Fort Whoop-Up and they searched it thoroughly, finding nothing.

The nearly abandoned state of Fort Whoop-Up all but proved Colonel French's theory that the traders were planning to wait out the mounted police. To confront the mounties was an unnecessary risk and there is not much to suggest that the whisky traders were long on courage. But Colonel French's decision to leave a force behind would prevent the traders' plan from succeeding. After the non-event at Fort Whoop-Up,

Jerry Potts led Colonel Macleod to an island on the Belly River (today known as the Old Man River) and there he and his men built their winter fort. It would be the first permanent mounted police stronghold on the southern prairie and would eventually bear the name Fort Macleod.

Discussions with the local First Nations began almost immediately. Colonel Macleod sent Jerry Potts to parlay with chiefs like Crowfoot of the Siksika, Red Crow of the Blood and Bull Head of the Peigan. Soon after, Macleod himself went to visit them in their camps, to explain why he and his men were in this territory, and what was expected of the Indians. From the beginning Colonel Macleod stressed that there would be one law for both white and Native, and that the mounted police meant to keep the promises they made. First Nations leaders approved both the plan and Macleod himself.

Colonel Macleod's ability to inspire confidence and trust in the First Nations people is well demonstrated by the story of how he came to have the Blackfoot name Stamixotokan, or Bull Head. The original Bull Head was a chief of the Peigan Nation and, because the first fort on the island upriver from Fort Whoop-Up was in Bull Head's hunting territory, Colonel Macleod visited him soon after the police arrival. So strongly affected was Bull Head by the manner and words of the Colonel that he gave him his own name. This meant that Bull Head had no name and must find another. He became known as Walking Forward.

A gallery of images from the History Television special "The Great March," depicting Fort Whoop-Up. The scenes were shot at the reconstructed Fort Whoop-Up on the Old Man River at Lethbridge, Alberta.

Jerry Potts in a familiar position: centered between the mounted police and the First Nations people.

All the mounted police troops made it to their destinations before the winter of 1874-75 set in. The greatest concentration (150 men) was at Fort Macleod with Colonel Macleod. "A" Division under Inspector Jarvis arrived safely at Fort Edmonton and stayed the winter there with the fur traders. Colonel French took his two divisions to the Fort Pelly/ Swan River area and left "E" Division to finish construction of the Swan River Barracks, which Ottawa had decreed the official mounted police headquarters in the west. Colonel French had orders not to return to Manitoba with any of his men, but he proceeded to do just that. He took Division "D" to Fort Dufferin and wintered there.

Chief Crowfoot of the Siksika Nation was one of the most influential leaders in the Blackfoot Confederacy. He welcomed the mounted police.

Chief Red Crow of the Blood Nation told the treaty negotiators of 1877 that Colonel Macleod had never told him a lie.

AFTER THE MARCH

(Inset) Henri Julien's drawing of a Sunday church service, and the depiction of a similar scene in "The Great March" television special. Each denomination had its own Sunday service, led by an officer of that religion.

Colonel James F. Macleod became the second Commissioner of the mounted police in 1876 when Colonel French was forced to resign. He was a popular choice.

The March West came very close to disaster, but the mounted police survived. By having Colonel Macleod and three divisions stay in the west, that narrow escape turned into a narrow success. The mounted police came west to halt the whisky trade and, if they did not stop it in their first winter in the west, they certainly slowed it down. Already by the summer of 1875, the Blackfoot were showing signs of renewed prosperity.

Now, with the march behind them, the mounted police had, if anything, a greater task ahead. The federal government had created the force to police the North-West Territories, in all their vast extent. The force must somehow spread itself thin enough to accomplish that.

Meanwhile, Colonel French's leadership was increasingly under fire. The independent style he showed when he disobeyed orders and returned to Manitoba for the winter, and his habit of engaging Ottawa in arguments over issues like the location of the Swan River Barracks, annoyed the powers that be. In July of 1876, after it had been recommended to Cabinet that French be replaced as Commissioner, he resigned.

This photo of NWMP officers at Fort Walsh in 1878 contains several notable figures from the early years. In the back row, second from the left, is Francis Jeffrey Dickens, the third son of the famous English novelist Charles Dickens. John McIllree (back row, third from the right) and Cecil Denny (back row, far right) left written accounts of the March West. Seated in the center row are Assistant-Commissioner Acheson Gosford Irvine (left), Commissioner Macleod (center) and Surgeon John Kittson (right). Kittson accompanied the Great March, trying to come up with antidotes to the prevalent dysentery and a means of warding off mosquitos.

Surgeon R.B. Nevitt's 1875 drawing of Fort Macleod. The fort was built on an Island
in what is now known as the Old Man River.

n the ranks of the mounted police, Colonel French had always had his enemies. Because several of them left diaries and wrote books, it is easy to forget he had his admirers too. As Colonel French and his wife prepared to leave the west, the men presented them with gifts: an expensive gold watch for the Colonel and a silver tea service for Mrs. French.

French's replacement as Commissioner was Colonel Macleod, who had to return to the force to accept the position. Six months previously he had left the mounties to devote his time to being stipendiary magistrate for the North-West Territories. Whatever side people were on in the French affair, they tended to approve the choice of Colonel Macleod as his replacement. One of Macleod's first decrees as Commissioner was to have mounted police headquarters moved from Swan River to Fort Macleod.

This reconstruction of Fort Edmonton is found a few miles upriver of the original site. After making their own incredible journey in the summer and fall of 1874, Inspector W.D. Jarvis and "A" Troop wintered at Fort Edmonton.

Fort Walsh, named for James Morrow Walsh, was built in 1875 not far from the site of the Cypress Hills Massacre.

By this time, several more forts had been added to the mounted police network. In 1875, Inspector Jarvis moved down river from Fort Edmonton and built Fort Saskatchewan. The same year, Inspector Walsh was sent with his "B" Division to build a fort in the Cypress Hills that he called Fort Walsh. In the summer of 1875, Inspector Brisebois took "F" Division and established another fort at the forks of the Bow and Elbow Rivers. Brisebois tried to follow Walsh's and Macleod's example and name the fort Brisebois, but the attempt was quickly countermanded by Macleod. Brisebois was an unpopular commander whose men almost mutinied in the early months at the Bow and Elbow. Colonel Macleod came up with a name for "F" Division's fort himself. After a place on the Macleod's ancestral Isle of Skye, he named it Fort Calgary.

In 1878, Fort Walsh became the new mounted police headquarters, replacing Fort Macleod. It held that position until 1882.

"E" Division on parade at Fort Calgary in 1883. Fort Calgary (inset) was built in 1875 at the confluence of the Bow and Elbow Rivers.

In 1876, another fort, called Battleford, was built on the North Saskatchewan between the fur trade posts of Pitt and Carlton, where the Battle River enters.

In the early years, it would be the mounties' often difficult job to help the First Nations people understand and deal with what history was sending their way. The first and hardest change was the near extermination of the buffalo. Indians who had long been enemies found themselves crowding together around the last herds, and at least once, those enemies considered joining to fight the white invasion of their land. Sitting Bull of the Sioux sent tobacco to Crowfoot of the Blackfoot asking him to join the Sioux in their war against the Americans. When they finished with them, they could deal with the white invasion north of the Medicine Line. But Crowfoot, at least in part because of the influence of the mounted police, declined.

79

Francis Jeffrey Dickens (1844-1886) was the third son of the famous British novelist Charles Dickens (author of Great Expectations, A Christmas Carol, Oliver Twist, etc.). After a stint in India's Bengal Mounted Police, "Frank" Dickens was appointed a Sub-Inspector with the Canadian Mounted Police on November 4, 1874, just as the March West was ending. As a mounted police officer he had a reputation for extravagance and questionable judgement. During the Northwest Rebellion of 1885, Dickens was in command of the mounted police at Ft. Pitt. After the Cree besieged the fort and demanded surrender, Dickens and his policemen waited until dawn and escaped down river to Battleford. In 1886, Dickens was discharged from the mounted police, because of deafness. A few months later, on the night he was to begin an American lecture tour, Frances Dickens died of a heart attack.

Detachment of N.W.M.P. at Fort Pitt. 1885.

Fort Pitt was a Hudson's Bay Company trading post but, in 1885, at the time of the North-West Rebellion, a detachment of mounted police was sent there under the leadership of Captain Francis Jeffrey Dickens (center foreground, under the # 12).

In this 1884 photograph, Cree Chief Big Bear (center left) is seen trading at Ft. Pitt. In 1885, during the North-West Rebellion, Big Bear would return to Pitt and place the fort under siege.

A basic cause of the North-West Rebellion was the sudden disappearance of the buffalo. After the buffalo had been killed for their hides, a secondary industry in horns, hooves and bones took over. The bones were shipped east by rail and ground for fertilizer and for use in sugar refining.

"The Stampede" by William Jacob Hays, from a time before the slaughter when the buffalo covered the plains for miles.

Sitting Bull was one of the military leaders of the Sioux during their war with the Americans in the 1870s. That war culminated in the defeat of General Custer at the Little Big Horn on June 25, 1876. Fugitive Sioux began crossing into Canada, in the Wood Mountain area later that year, and Sitting Bull himself came in 1877.

The mounted police could do little, however, to help the First Nations people of Canada when starvation loomed, and the possibility of armed resistance would return again and again in the 1870s and '80s.

In 1876, Sitting Bull's Sioux defeated General Custer and the 7th Cavalry at the Little Big Horn. By the spring of 1877, many lodges of fugitive Sioux had entered Canada seeking sanctuary and were learning how differently Canada's mounted police would treat them. The Sioux entered Canada near

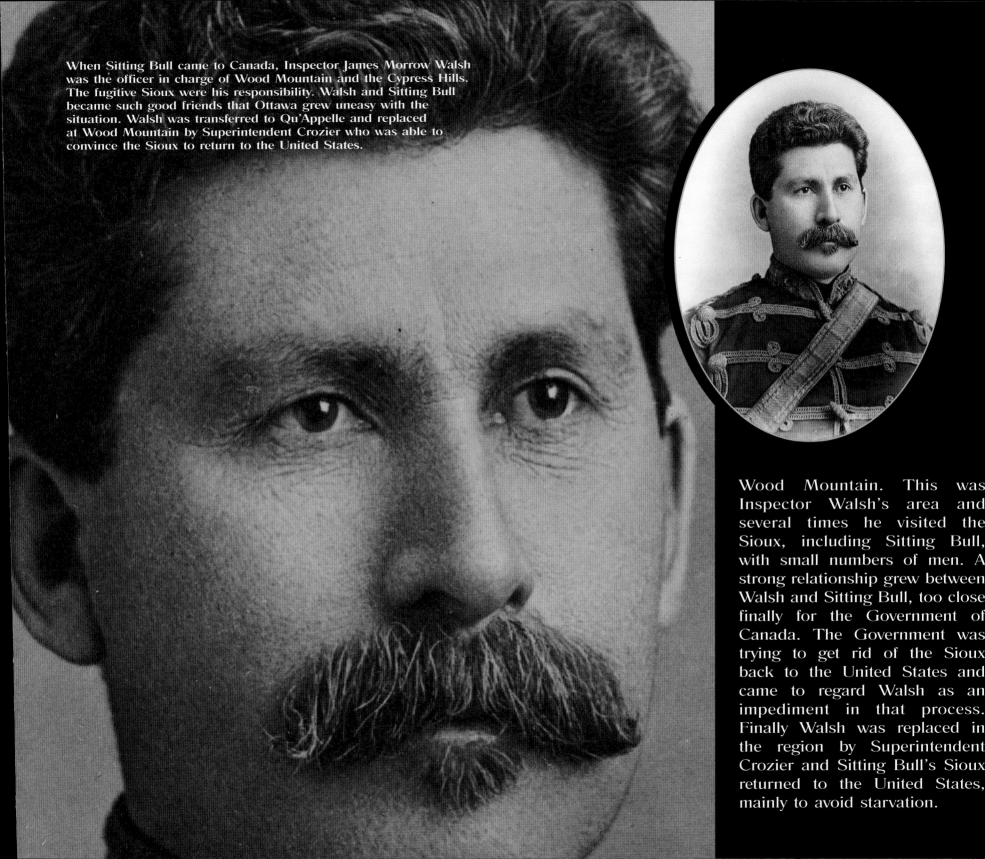

When Sitting Bull came to Canada, Inspector James Morrow Walsh was the officer in charge of Wood Mountain and the Cypress Hills. The fugitive Sioux were his responsibility. Walsh and Sitting Bull became such good friends that Ottawa grew uneasy with the situation. Walsh was transferred to Qu'Appelle and replaced at Wood Mountain by Superintendent Crozier who was able to convince the Sioux to return to the United States.

Wood Mountain. This was Inspector Walsh's area and several times he visited the Sioux, including Sitting Bull, with small numbers of men. A strong relationship grew between Walsh and Sitting Bull, too close finally for the Government of Canada. The Government was trying to get rid of the Sioux back to the United States and came to regard Walsh as an impediment in that process. Finally Walsh was replaced in the region by Superintendent Crozier and Sitting Bull's Sioux returned to the United States, mainly to avoid starvation.

Robert Magee's "In the Land of the Mounted Police" shows Assistant Commissioner Irvine, Inspector Walsh and three others entering the Sioux camp for a parlay with Sitting Bull.

Robert Magee

Robert Magee

In Robert Magee's painting "Blackfoot Crossing," the mounted police meet First Nations people, including Chief Crowfoot (foreground, right), during the Treaty # 7 negotiations in 1877.

The Canadian Government used the good relationship that existed between the mounted police and the First Nations people during the great treaty negotiations in the west. The building of Fort Battleford was a preparation for Treaty # 6 with the Saskatchewan Indians (Cree and Assiniboine). In 1876, the mounties provided an escort for the treaty commissioners at Fort Carlton. In September of 1877, the process was repeated for the Mountain Assiniboine and Blackfoot Confederacy tribes at Blackfoot Crossing east of Fort Calgary.

This was Treaty # 7 and 108 mounted policemen participated. In their speeches at Treaty # 7, several chiefs mentioned how much they appreciated the work of the mounted police. Crowfoot said the mounted police protected his people the way a bird's feathers protect it in winter. Red Crow said he had never known Stamixotokan (Colonel Macleod) to lie. Obviously the trust built up by the mounted police had a lot to do with the willingness of most chiefs to sign.

In this painting of the Treaty # 7 ceremonies at Blackfoot Crossing in 1877, artist Archibald Bruce Stapleton depicts Chief Crowfoot giving a speech to the Queen's representatives. The mounted police were present in strength, and their good reputation with the Blackfoot Confederacy Nations weighed heavily in the Queen's and Canada's favor.

Artillery drill at the NWMP barracks in Regina, 1885.

Not long after, in 1879, the mounted police received their first official name. They became the North-West Mounted Police.

The 1880s brought a crisis that mounted police good will, diplomacy and fair play could not defuse. Simply, the buffalo were gone and many white people were entering the lands that the Natives and Métis had controlled for a very long time. When the railway crossed the prairie in the early '80s, the Native people did what they could to slow its progress. Piapot camped on the right of way and it was the duty of mounted police Constable W.B. Wilde to remove him.

Mounted police guarding the courthouse in Regina during Louis Riel's trial for treason.

At Ft. Walsh, in 1879, Constable Fred Young and Corporal G.B. Moffat pose for two very different photographs against the same log wall backdrop. On the left, they appear in their NWMP dress uniforms. In the center, they give the folks back home a wild-west frontiersman view. Nor was dressing up frontier-style for the camera restricted to the lower ranks. The desperado on the right is Inspector James Morrow Walsh.

THE EARLY YEARS

NWMP headquarters moved to the Territorial Capital of Regina in 1882. The building in the background is the riding school where recruits could learn the fine art of equitation year round.

"Depot Division," Regina as it appears today. Although the force headquarters moved to Ottawa in 1920, the Cadet Training Academy remains at Depot Division. The RC added in 1973. Note the steepled RCMP chapel in the lower left-hand quadrant; the oldest existing building in Regina.

When Regina became the headquarters of the NWMP in 1882, "B" Division moved there from Ft. Walsh.

After the construction of the Canadian Pacific Railway, the balance of population in the west changed quickly. Métis and First Nations people became a minority. New towns were sprinkled along the railway right-of-way and one of them, Regina, was declared the capital of the North-West Territories. In 1882, the headquarters of the NWMP were moved to that capital. By 1883, the number of mounties had increased to 500 and the number of divisions had dropped to five. Forts Macleod, Battleford and Calgary were home to Divisions "C," "D," and "E," respectively. "B" Division, Inspector Walsh's old troop at Cypress Hills, had moved to HQ in Regina. "A" was centered at Maple Creek. There were many more sub-posts, or detachments: several per division.

An aerial view of the Saskatchewan Legislature. Before becoming the Capital of Saskatchewan in 1905, Regina was chosen Capital of the North-West Territories in 1883.

Ft. Calgary (inset) became a divisional post in 1882 and Division "E" was transferred there. Ft. Macleod was the divisional post for "C" Troop (main photo).

NWMP at Banff in 1880. Sled dogs were the winter means of travel
for mounted police in many western and northern locales.

A NWMP group at Donald Station, B.C. in the winter of 1884-5.

THE HOMESTEADER'S FRIEND

This photograph of a mounted policeman with a homestead family and a local clergyman typifies mounted police duties during the settlement rush on the prairies from 1890 to 1910.

During the ranching era and the prairie settlement boom, mounted police work involved long days of riding from one settler's cabin to the next.

As the settlement wave rolled across the west, mounted police detachments were often the social and communications hub for fledgling communities. Up until 1883, many detachments doubled as postal depots. On special occasions, the police hosted gala evenings to which the local civilians were invited. When the settlement boom reached its peak, the mounted police guided homesteaders to available land, kept records on soil conditions, reported on crops, and fought prairie fires. In every way, the mounted police were the settler's friends.

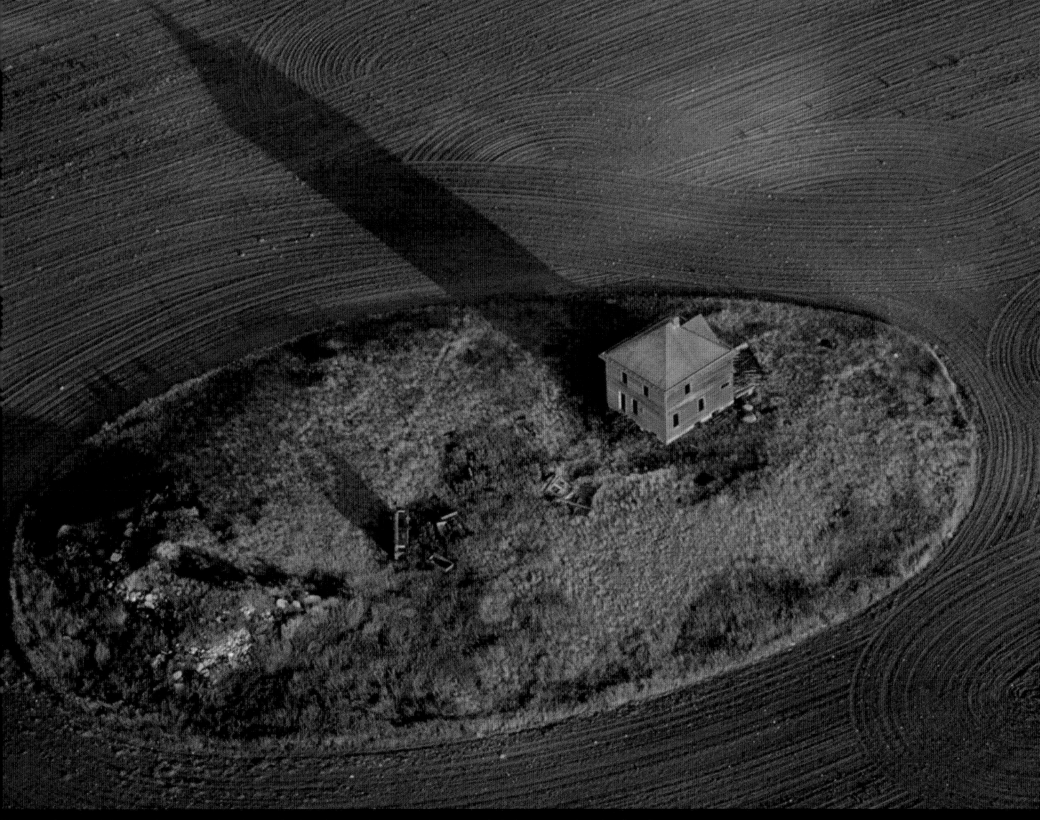
This modern aerial view shows an abandoned Saskatchewan homestead; surrounded, but respected, by the plow.

the railway progressed westward, policing problems ved with it. For the final leg of construction ough the mountains, Sam Steele, now an Inspector, s asked to form a detachment with which to police Two major strikes by railway construction workers vided the biggest challenge and, during the second ke in 1885, Sam Steele added to his legend by ving bed during an illness to stand before a mob who re trying to prevent an arrest. The Riot Act was read, eele threatened violence, and the strikers dispersed.

was the job of the NWMP to police the construction of the Canadian Pacific Railway.

Inspector Sam Steele and company at the Beaver River camp on the CPR line. It was here that construction workers took advantage of the North- West Rebellion of 1885 to go on strike over unpaid wages. Steele was in bed with Rocky Mountain Fever but, when a riot threatened, he armed himself, faced the strikers and restored peace.

In the 1890s, the tradition of northern Canadian patrols began among the mounted police. In 1895, Inspector Charles Constantine led a party of mounted policemen up the Pacific Coast to the mouth of the Yukon River in Alaska, and then up the Yukon 1,500 miles until they had entered Canadian territory (the future Yukon Territory). There they built Fort Constantine, the northernmost fort in the British Empire. When gold was discovered further upriver at Bonanza Creek, Fort Constantine was extremely useful and was supplemented by Fort Herchmer in 1897 closer to the gold fields of Dawson Creek. As gold seekers poured in from all around the world - making fortunes, going broke - the NWMP kept the peace, collected customs duties, and spread its traditions of policing and justice across a new frontier.

NWMP Custom House at the top of the Chilkoot Pass on Alaska-B.C. border, 1898. An estimated 20,000 to 30,000 people climbed the pass en route to the Yukon Territory during the Klondike Gold Rush.

A tent detachment at Lake Bennett, on the main route to Dawson City and the Yukon gold fields, 1898.

A NWMP street guard at Whitehorse, Yukon, on Victoria Day, ca. 1900.

Policing the gold rush was an early step in the policing of Canada's north by the NWMP.

Members of "M" Division at Fort Fullerton on the west coast of Hudson's Bay, 1904. Superintendent J.D. Moodie is 3rd from the left in the front row, behind the man seated in the snow in foreground.

A mounted police patrol leaves Dawson for Herschel Island in the Mackenzie Delta. Dec. 27, 1904.

The turn of the 20th century brought with it several changes for the mounted police. In 1904, their name was changed again. King Edward VII conferred the prefix "Royal" to the NWMP so that it became the RNWMP (Royal North-West Mounted Police). In 1905, the North-West Territories changed radically when Alberta and Saskatchewan were accorded the status of Provinces. The mounted police provided the new provinces with their policing.

The thrust into the far north continued. In 1903, Sergeant F.J. Fitzgerald sailed in a whaling boat to Herschel Island beyond the mouth of the Mackenzie Delta. In the same year, a mounted police post, Fort Fullerton, was established high on the western shore of Hudson's Bay. In 1907-08, Inspector E.A. Pelletier conducted a 24 month, 3,347 mile patrol that linked the western and eastern Arctic. From Fort Saskatchewan near Edmonton, he traveled overland to Fort Fullerton and then south to Gimli, Manitoba.

A RNWMP search party prepares to leave Dawson on Feb. 28, 1911. The "Lost Patrol" left Fort McPherson for Dawson on Dec. 21, 1910, and never arrived.

The incredible northern patrols of the RNWMP were not always successful. In 1910, three mounted policemen and a recently retired ex-mounted police guide froze to death after becoming lost between Fort McPherson and Dawson Creek.

A mounted police Arctic patrol returning to Dawson on Mar. 17, 1913.

#9, July 16, 1908. R.N.W.M.P. tent. Fort McPherson, Peel River.
Ahcuk. Constable Frank Pearson. Sergt. Selig. "Rory" Memeganna (Interpreter)

RNWMP squadron under Superintendent Warsley, preparing for deployment to Vladivostok, Russia in 1918.

Time of war meant a difficult choice for the military-minded mounties. In 1899, over 200 mounted policemen were given leave to fight in the Boer War. When the Canadian Government refused to allow mounties to volunteer for service in the First World War, the decision was very unpopular. In 1918, the decree was reversed and over 700 RNWMP were given leave to enlist. A group of mounted police were also sent to Siberia as part of a plan to resist Russia's Bolshevik revolution. The drain on manpower eventually brought the mounties down to 303 men, close to the original 1874 complement. Another change during this period saw Saskatchewan and Alberta create provincial police forces to police their provincial laws.

113

RNWMP officers at Shorncliffe, England, 1918. Note that their uniforms are army uniforms rather than RNWMP uniforms.

In this "fashion show," one sees the full range of RNWMP uniforms.

By the end of the First World War, the RNWMP were in charge of enforcing federal laws in Manitoba, Saskatchewan, Alberta and British Columbia, and were in charge of all policing in the North-West Territories and Yukon Territory. But starting in 1919, with a report from Commissioner A. Bowen Perry, the mounted police underwent a fundamental change that would transform them from a western and northern unit into a national and international one. The modern RCMP began to emerge.

The RCMP

Members of Canada's Dominion Police doing desk work in Ottawa, 1909.

On February 1st, 1920, Canada's mounted police took on the name by which they are known today: the Royal Canadian Mounted Police (RCMP). The name change was part of a major re-organization that included the absorption of Canada's Dominion Police. The RCMP became Canada's sole federal police force

operating coast to coast. New RCMP divisions were created in many Canadian cities and some of the old divisional headquarters, like Fort Macleod and Fort Battleford, became detachments. The mounties left their attractive headquarters in Regina and took up residence in Ottawa.

The NWMP band at the newly-opened Banff Springs Hotel in 1888. Bandmaster, Staff Sergeant Fred Bagley is in the center of the photo, directly under the bass drum in the center of the middle row.

THE '74 MOUNTIES

After the March of 1874, the mounted police force expanded rapidly to meet the obligations of its huge mandate. But the early members of the force, the veterans who endured the difficult trek from Ft. Dufferin west, were not forgotten. They became known as the "'74 Mounties," and were often honoured on special occasions in the West they had helped transform. In the panoramic photo above, many of the '74 Mounties are gathered for their role in the original Calgary Stampede of 1912. In the group photo on the right, several of them gather on the steps of the Palliser Hotel as part of Calgary's Jubilee Celebration. Age has begun to tell on the '74 Mounties but they are still a proud, fine-looking group of men.

n front of Calgary's City Hall in 1925, on the occasion of the Calgary Jubilee (its 50th year), March West veterans posed for this photograph.
Fred Bagley is in the middle row, 3rd from the left.

RNWMP group at Dawson, Yukon, 1914. Photo by J. Doody.

In the 1920s, the RCMP was given the task of establishing Canadian sovereignty over a remote and disputed wilderness, not unlike their original role on the western prairies. This time it was Canada's High Arctic where Danes and Greenland Inuit were hunting without Canadian permission. To enforce Canada's territorial claims in the area, the mounted police were sent north to establish permanent posts on Ellesmere, Baffin and Devon Islands.

Official opening of the mounted police Detachment at Dundas Harbour, NWT, 1924.

Northern Patrols have been a fact of mounted police life since the late 19th century.

The "Distributor" lands at Ft. Norman, NWT, 1925.

RCMP Constable T.H. Tredgold poses with an Inuit family at Cumberland Gulf, Baffin Island, ca. 1924-7.

A patrol at Eldorado Camp, Great Bear Lake, 1931.

Inspector Dolphin looks on as his sleigh runners are de-iced at Union Straight, 1931.

At Twin Glacier, NWT, 1953, RCMP Special Constable Minkyoo (left), his wife and child (right) and RCMP Constable Ed Jones

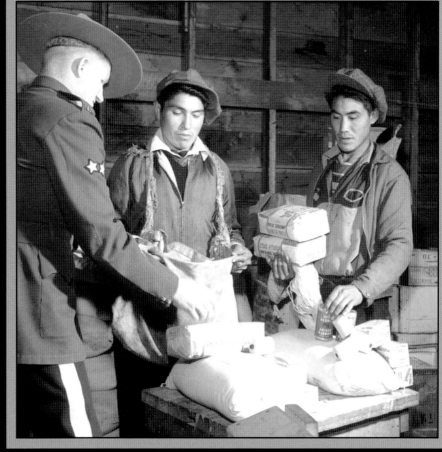

At Fort Good Hope, NWT, in 1953, RCMP Constable W.H. Christianson assembles flour, sugar and fishing net twine for distribution

In the 20th century, the Royal North West Mounted Police began to trade their horses in for cars and motorcycles. This photo was taken at Boissevain, Manitoba in 1917.

While the northern patrols and northern posts were in the old mounted police tradition, police duties in the south were changing rapidly with the character of the country. With the illegal liquor trade of the Prohibition and the illegal drug traffic of later years, the RCMP was fighting organized crime. Scientific detection methods (ballistics, forensics, fingerprinting, etc.) and high performance radio-equipped automobiles and boats were the only hope of success. About the time the horse became obsolete in RCMP police work, the force took to the air. For a time, they borrowed planes from the Royal Canadian Air Force but, starting in 1937, they bought their own.

After borrowing planes from the RCAF in the early '30s, the RCMP acquired its own air fleet of de Havilland Rapide aircraft in 1937. The aircraft in this picture carry "custom" Canadian civil registrations with a two letter reference (MP) to their police purpose. The ultra-modern Pilatus PC-12 aircraft depicted on page 136 carries the identical CF-MPA registration as one of the aircraft above. Maintaining these historical registrations has become a Mountie tradition.

An RCMP motorcycle policeman posed in front of Mt. Rundle in Banff National Park.

The RCMP's floating detachment and supply vessel St. Roch was built in North Vancouver in 1928. By a two-year voyage from Vancouver to Halifax, ending on October 11th, 1942, she became the first vessel to navigate the Northwest Passage from the Pacific to the Atlantic. The St. Roch's return voyage from Halifax to Vancouver in 1944 was completed in an incredible 86 days. In 1950, the RCMP's legendary ship chalked up another first when she sailed from Vancouver to Halifax via the Panama Canal, becoming the first ship to circumnavigate the North American continent. The St. Roch was retired in 1954 and is a featured attraction at the Vancouver Maritime Museum.

The RCMP supply vessel St. Roch challenged northern Canada's formidable Northwest Passage in 1941-2 and again in 1944. In this photo, the St. Roch is anchored at Herschel Island in the Beaufort Sea.

The St. Roch, taking on fresh water.

The St. Roch, locked in the ice in Franklin Strait. Inset photo: the St. Roch's captain, Sergeant Henry A. Larsen.

A return to provincial policing began in 1928 when Saskatchewan disbanded its provincial police force and established a new contract system for utilizing the RCMP. This contract model was used when other provinces (Alberta, Manitoba, New Brunswick, Nova Scotia and Prince Edward Island) made the same choice in the 1930s. British Columbia and the new province of Newfoundland contracted the RCMP for provincial policing in 1950. Only Quebec and Ontario retained provincial police services.

By the beginning of the Second World War, the transformation into a modern police force was well on its way. The mounted police secret service had already penetrated most Nazi and Fascist organizations in Canada and, within hours of the declaration of war against Germany, hundreds of Nazi sympathizers were arrested.

For this war, a 125-man Division (No. 1, Provost Company, RCMP) was recruited to represent the mounted police in the fighting overseas. Women took over many administrative positions to alleviate the human resource shortage. The marine and air services were transferred to the war effort for the duration of the conflict.

In the Second World War, No. 1 Provost Company, RCMP, a 125-man Division of RCMP was formed to fight overseas. Here, a group from No. 1 Provost Company poses at Aldershot, England in 1940.

The post-war RCMP grew rapidly, as did the nation, and, by 1960, RCMP personnel numbered 7,558. Of these, 596 were civilian members and 1,049 were civil servants.

Over time, the RCMP has become a comprehensive national police service. In addition to policing federal laws across the land, it provides provincial police service on contract to all provinces except Ontario and Quebec. The force continues to police Canada's northern territories and has contracts to police 198 Canadian municipalities. Internationally, Canada has been a member of Interpol since 1949. Through Interpol, the RCMP cooperates with police services all over the world to pursue criminals and to combat international crime.

RCMP officers checking motorists, 1957.

Women became regular members of the RCMP in 1974. The first female commissioned officers came on the scene in 1992.

After decades in the security service business, the force handed this function over to a separate agency, the Canadian Security Intelligence Service (CSIS), in 1984. As of July 30, 1997, the RCMP employed 21,443 persons. Of that total, 14,878 were regular members of the force. Civilian members and public servants made up 6,236.

In 1874, the mounted police traveled by horse and conveyed their goods by wagon and ox-cart. One hundred and twenty-five years later, the equivalent is an array of powerful land, water, snow and air vehicles: everything from radar-equipped marine patrol vessels to snowmobiles and helicopters.

The continuing modernization of the force has necessarily meant intensive computerization. The Canadian Police Information Centre (CPIC) is a central data bank available through 2,500 access points Canada-wide. Data available include descriptions of criminal suspects, missing persons and stolen cars and property; as well as fingerprints, dental records and files on persons inclined to wander and endanger themselves (such as those suffering from Alzheimer's Disease). Computers and telecommunication systems are also employed to combat illegal uses of themselves: the new wave of computer and telecommunication theft and fraud.

The RCMP's earliest commitment was to Canada's Aboriginal People. Several of the latest innovations in RCMP policing are attempts to improve the RCMP-First Nations relationship. The recruitment of Aboriginal Canadians as members of the force has been a priority throughout the 1990s. Negotiation of policing agreements with Aboriginal communities is another way the force is trying to respond to First Nations wants, needs and culture.

Helicopters and airplanes have greatly improved the RCMP's ability to police and aid Canadians living in remote locations. Above photo: Bell 206 Jet Ranger helicopters display both 1980's and 1990's paint schemes.

At the end of the millennium, the de Havilland DHC-6 Twin Otter, a classic Canadian bush aircraft, is being phased out of service after decades of reliable operation in extreme weather conditions.

A newly-acquired Pilatus aircraft overflies the skyline of Hull, Québec on its way to the RCMP hangar at Ottawa's airport.
The ultra-high-tech Pilatus PC-12 represents the cutting edge of aviation technology and the RCMP's commitment to providing service to all parts of Canada.

Through all this modernization, the RCMP has been careful not to lose sight of its origins. The force established a Historical Branch in 1968 and opened its Centennial Museum in Regina in 1973. To keep the word "mounted" in its title, the RCMP maintains its famed Musical Ride. The Ride dates back all the way to the 1870s and was the subject of a Frederic Remington drawing in an 1887 Harper's Weekly. The Ride was dropped during the World War II period, then brought back, bigger and better than ever, in 1948. The post-war ride featured coal black horses in fulfillment of then-Commissioner Wood's dream of how fine the mounted police scarlet would look in contrast to all-black mounts. To ensure horses of uniform size and color, the force established its own breeding ranch, originally at Fort Walsh in the Cypress Hills of Saskatchewan, then moved to Pakenham, Ontario in 1968. Her Majesty Queen Elizabeth II has been presented with three RCMP Musical Ride horses as gifts: "Burmese," "Centennial" and, recently, "James." Every year, the RCMP Musical Ride tours Canada and responds to invitations from all over the world. As well as being a globally popular spectacle, it is one of the most sought after tours of duty for mounted police, with a waiting list of over 600. (Another popular unit is the handling of police service German and Belgian Shepherds with a waiting list of 400.)

The Musical Ride is one of the most popular tours of duty for the women and men of the Royal Canadian Mounted Police.

The Royal Canadian Mounted Police Musical Ride is a welcome and popular attraction all over the world.

A popular police force may seem to many a contradiction in terms, but, in Canada, the RCMP approaches that. Just as it did in its relations with the First Nations people during the 1870s, the modern force does not let desire for popularity bend it away from strict enforcement of the law. It prefers to gain popularity through consistency and fairness.

The old principles of honesty and one law look as good today as they did to the First Nations people in 1874. Add to that the incredible courage displayed during the March West and during the famous Arctic patrols of later years, and the sum is a legacy that all Canadians can look to as a source of pride and inspiration. As Canada moves into a new Millennium, the history of the mounted police reminds us how we came to be a nation that places fairness above territoriality and momentary politics. Like the mounted police of 1874, Canada marches forward into the future armed with sound ideals, strengthened by courage.

The End

"The Graduation"

James Lumbers '97

OF THE MARCH WEST

Volunteers in period mounted police uniforms hold up the RCMP/ GRC 125th Anniversary banner.

In celebration of the 125th Anniversary of the founding of the force, the RCMP's 125th Anniversary Committee scheduled commemorative events throughout Canada and internationally in 1998 and 1999. The grand finale of the 125th festivities is the live re-enactment of the March West in the summer of 1999.

Crew setting up crane shot of Henri Julien (Matthew McHugh).

Art Director Drew Moreau listens intently to instructions for staging the next shot while the recruits take a break.

In collaboration with the RCMP, General Assembly Production Centre (GAPC) of Ottawa also produced a 2-hour documentary entitled The North West Mounted Police: The Great March. GAPC sent a motion picture crew to the Grassy Lakes area of southern Alberta near Lethbridge to shoot dramatic "elements for this History Television special about the March West of

1874. Many of John McQuarrie's photographs featured in this book published by GAPC, were shot on the set of "The Great March".

The motion picture portion of the 125th anniversary celebration is the latest in a long tradition of movie depictions of the

Camp scene during location shooting near Lethbridge, Alberta.

Brave recruits shed their uniforms for a frosty October dip in the river.

mounted police dating back to 1910 when the Edison Moving Picture Company featured mounties in a silent feature called "Riders of the Plains." Over the years, the Canadian mounted policeman became something of a movie staple in the United States. Tom Mix, Nelson Eddy, Robert Preston, Alan Ladd, George O'Brian, Paul Gross and Lee Marvin are just a few of the American actors who have appeared as movie mounties. Nelson Eddy as a mountie singing to, and with, Jeanette MacDonald in 1936's "Rose Marie" was a particular hit that spawned several more mountie epics on the silver screen.

The Canadian film and television industry eventually got into the act of packaging mounties for pop culture consumption. A good example is the hit television series "Due South" in which Albertan Paul Gross plays Benton Fraser, an RCMP officer on special assignment with his German Shepherd "Diefenbaker" to fight crime on the streets of Chicago.

GAPC's "The Great March" is somewhat different in that it attempts to "show it like it was" on the inaugural march of 1874. Without a Steven Spielberg-sized budget, showing it like it was is no mean feat. The production team, commissioned by GAPC Entertainment executive producer Marcel Clément, consisted of producer Hoda Elatawi, director Roger Cardinal, and directors of photography Ian McLaren and Louis Durocher. They were able to weave their magic with the assistance of horsemen from the Lethbridge area, people from the Peigan Nation, Métis from Rocky

Steadicam operator Jeff Cools and Director Roger Cardinal discuss next set-up, while first camera assistant Richard Venasse prepares the camera.

Producer Hoda Elatawi and Director Roger Cardinal solve a problem while "recruits" patiently wait for the next direction.

Mountain House and a group of RCMP volunteers. White Iron Productions of Calgary provided extraordinary crew support through production manager Doug Burquist. Artifacts for the re-enactment were supplied by Parks Canada and the RCMP's Centennial Museum in Regina.

The script for the special was written by Calgarian Fred Stenson, based as much as possible on diaries, letters and memoirs written by the original mounted police. Jean D'Artigue of France was a 22 year old schoolteacher when he presented himself at a mounted police recruiting office in 1874. His highly critical Six Years in the Canadian North-West was the first book ever published by a force member. Fred Bagley, who served with the original mounties as a 15 year old trumpeter left an often humorous and wonderfully detailed unpublished memoir, much of which is devoted to the march. Other excellent sources include the diary and official

Trooper recruit receives hair cut prior to filming.

Setting up for a scene at Writing on Stone Provincial Park.

report of Colonel French, the reports written by reporter/artist Henri Julien who was assigned to cover the march for the Canadian Illustrated News, the diary of Sub-Constable Joseph Carscadden and the memoirs of James Walker, Sam Steele and Cecil Denny. Peigan elder Reg Crowshoe and several historians appear in the TV special, providing analysis and perspective.

The airing of the "The Great March" on History Television (and subsequently Société Radio-Canada and the Saskatchewan Communication Network) helps to usher in the real-life re-enactment. Starting in Emerson, Manitoba on May 8th, 1999, serving and retired members of the RCMP, wearing vintage uniforms, retrace the steps of the mounted policemen of 1874. A changing cast of uniformed and un-uniformed riders and teamsters from the community join them over the 56 day journey. The

Executive producer, Marcel Clément on location with John McQuarrie for book photo shoot.

March is really two marches: a northern route, from Beardy's Okemasis First Nation in Saskatchewan to Fort Saskatchewan, near Edmonton, in Alberta; and a southern route, from Emerson, Manitoba (Fort Dufferin) to Fort Macleod, Alberta. The latter trek covers 1500 kilometres. The RCMP Musical Ride joins the march and gives performances at several key locations, and First Nations communities are invited to join the march for Pow-Wows and smoke ceremonies.

On video and on horseback the RCMPs 125th anniversary celebration is a grand reminder of how this fledgling nation spread its wings in the final decades of the 19th century; a reminder too of our shared history with the Métis and First Nations people whose cultures are older than the Royal Canadian Mounted Police, older than Canada.

GAPC
ENTERTAINMENT
PRESENTS

THE NORTH-WEST MOUNTED POLICE
THE GREAT MARCH

A Television Documentary Special

Credits
Executive Producers
Marcel Clément
Kenneth Stewart

Producers
Hoda Elatawi
Marcel Clément

Director
Roger Cardinal

Creative Director
Ron Allen

Writer
Fred Stenson

Original Score by
Andrew Huggett

Executive Producer for
History Television
Sydney Suissa

RCMP Coordinator
Greg Peters

Alberta Coordinating Assistance
White Iron Productions
Michael Herringer

Narration
Neil Shee

Character Voices
Rick Jones

We wish to acknowledge the generous participation of the people of the city of Lethbridge and surrounding areas who so freely gave their time and enthusiasm to this production:

Cast

Col. George Arthur French
Cpl. Jerry McCarty

Henri Julien
Matthew McHugh

Fred Bagley
Patrick Walsh Jr.

Colonel James Macleod
Don Engel

Sub-Cst. Joseph Carscadden
Allen Kelly

Jerry Potts
Bill Sanders

Native Chief
Reg Crow Shoe

Pierre Leveillé
Sgt. Jay Weibe

Extras

Cheyenne Allison
Cst. Paul Benoit
Cyril Bertsch
Bill Bier
Jesse Bird
Dan Card
Lon Carlson
Sgt. Wayne Carroll
Andrew Cartwright
Matthew Clement
David Cormican
Amelia Crow Shoe
Anita Crow Shoe
Anthony Crow Shoe
Chris Crow Shoe
Karli Crow Shoe
Troy Crow Shoe
Norm Davies
Doran Degenstei
Ralph Dillenbeck
Jason Dobirstein
Keith Drews
Michael Fenton
Clement Fox
Bryce Francom
Tim Gallant
Terry Gates
Jeff Israelson
Gerry Karchuk
Wade Karchuk
Douglas Kast
Frank Kast

Peter King
George F. Kush
Charles Layton
Mark Layton
Stanford Little Plume
Brian McKenzie
Garry McLeod
Cor Ment
Eric E. Nystrom
Robin Pahl
Tyrone Potts
Lucien Prairie Chicken
Tim Roth
Harold Rutledge
Joey Savidant
Dave Shaver
Jessie Scott
Ranken Shimazaki
Brian L. Shockey
Bryan Smith
Gail Whitson
Bill Sanders
Eugene Torrie
Luke Torrie
Spencer Torrie
Murray Turner
Pat Walsh Sr.
David Walters
Serene Weasel Traveller
Tommy Werner
Thomas Yellow Face

First Unit Crew

Production manager/1st ad
Douglas Berquist

Director of photography
Ian Matheson

1st camera assistant
Richard Venasse

Steadicam operator
Jeff Cools

Jib operator
Bill Bruvold

Key grip
Alan Belyea

Gaffer
Jim Greggor

Best boy/swing
Jim Hurd

Sound mixer
Ron Osiowy

Art director
Drew Moreau

Props assistants
Tom Carroll
Robin Pahl

Script continuity
Madeleine Rozon

Make-up/hair
Pat Engstrom

Assistant make-up/hair
Marilyn Riddoch

Wardrobe
Momentum Design Ltd.

Production assistant/2nd ad
Colin Allen

Production coordinator
Liliane Day

Production assistants
Katie Brooker
Nic Dieterle

Production assistant/driver
Sarah Carroll

Production stills
John McQuarrie

Helicopter pilot
Ron Allard/Turbo West

RCMP technical advisors
Dr. Bill Beahen
Allen Burchill,
Assistant Commissioner (Retired)
Glenn Wright

RCMP location coordination
Sgt. Wayne Carroll
Cst. Don Vincent
Sgt. Jay Weibe

Location wranglers
Cpl. Jerry McCarty
Sgt. Jay Weibe
Eugene Torrie

On a warm summer evening, a giant Mountie and his charger drift silently across the grounds of "N" Division in Ottawa. As Colonel French and the intrepid '74 Mounties worked their way across the "great lone land", they could hardly have imagined that, 125 years later, a six storey hot air balloon in the shape of a Mountie on horseback would lift into the setting sun over Ottawa in celebration of what they had started. Nor could they have pictured the thousands of Canadians who can be seen waiting below (upper left) for the members of the Musical Ride to begin the "Sunset Ceremony". This equitation spectacle traces its roots back across the pages of this book to the men of the Great March. Far below, as the Commissioner stands ready to take the salute from "The Ride", the spirit of Colonel French and his men blows on the wind. They would be so proud.

The March West
Image Credits

Glenbow Museum Archives, Calgary

Glenbow Museum Archives, Calgary - Henri Julien Drawings

National Archives of Canada

Provincial Archives of Manitoba

Montana Historical Society, Helena

RCMP Air Section

Paintings by Robert Magee

Pierre St-Jacques, Imagination Photo Services

Paintings by James Lumbers Publishing Ltd.

John McQuarrie Photography

David Walters

Mike Reno

GAPC

Christine Bisson

David H. O'Malley